THE
COLLECTED POEMS OF
ARTHUR YAP

THE
COLLECTED POEMS OF
ARTHUR YAP

WITH AN INTRODUCTION BY
IRVING GOH

NUS PRESS
SINGAPORE

Published by:
NUS PRESS
National University of Singapore
AS3-01-02, 3 Arts Link, Singapore 117569

Fax: (65) 6774-0652
E-mail: nusbooks@nus.edu.sg
Website: http://nuspress.nus.edu.sg

ISBN 978-9971-69-653-5 (paperback)
First edition 2013
Reprint 2017

National Library Board, Singapore Cataloguing-in-Publication Data

Yap, Arthur.
    The collected poems of Arthur Yap / Arthur Yap ; with an introduction
    by Irving Goh. – Singapore: NUS Press, [2013]
    270 pages, 216 x 140mm

    I. Goh, Irving. II. Title.
    PR9570.S53
    S821 -- dc23   OCN807039032

Front Image by: Arthur Yap
Designed and typeset by: Sarah and Schooling
Printed by: Mainland Press Pte Ltd

With the Support of:

NATIONAL ARTS COUNCIL
SINGAPORE

In memory of Arthur Yap

叶纬雄

1943 – 2006

.

CONTENTS

THIS COLLECTION PRESENTS every published poem of Arthur Yap. We have proposed to present them in reverse chronological order. Poems from the early collections such as *commonplace* (1977) and *down the line* (1980) have been read, studied, appreciated, and cited countless times, by poetry lovers and literary scholars alike. With the reverse chronology, we would like to bring attention to Arthur's later poems, especially those written around 2001, which are no less interesting and written with no less poetic dexterity.

The collection begins therefore with the three poems that were given to *Quarterly Literary Review Singapore* in 2001 (with "mixed shots" published posthumously only in 2008), the poem "sociability" written in 2000, and the nine poems that were given to *Straits Times Life!* in 2001, where they were published as the "vignettes" (and we note here that "this boy's zoo" in the "vignettes" series was first titled "the boy's zoo" in Arthur's manuscript, and published as "this girl's zoo" in *AWARENESS*). For readers familiar with Arthur's earlier works, we hope these poems will not only be a pleasant surprise but also something that will provide them with a fresh perspective on his oeuvre. For readers who are newly initiated into his poetry here, we do hope these poems will indeed form a path towards a discovery of his poetic genius—a more veritable and exciting discovery perhaps than beginning with his more "representative" poems, of which so much has already been said.

The 2001 poems are followed by those published in the collection *man snake apple & other poems* (1986). Like the 2001 poems, we do think the poems in this collection deserve greater attention and appreciation. They are no doubt more difficult than the poems in *down the line* or *commonplace*, but it is perhaps with poems such as "tropical paradise" and "man snake apple" that give Arthur's poetry the depth or *pathos* matching those, we dare say, of T. S. Eliot's *The Waste Land* and *Four Quartets*. As with the poems published in 2001 and after, we have chosen to use the lowercase for the poems' titles in *man snake apple*, which were in capitals in the original collection. We believe the lowercase is Arthur's preference, as evident in the collection of selected poems, *the space of city trees* (2000), where all the titles were in the lowercase.

The poems from Arthur's "major" collections *down the line*, *commonplace*, and *only lines* (1971) are certainly included here. Some readers might well remember that *commonplace* also included a series of Arthur's paintings titled *black and white*. We did intend to reproduce them here. However, we no longer have the complete series, and therefore decided to leave them out. But back to the poems themselves: perhaps there will be one more pleasant surprise for the reader as he or she peruses the earlier collections. Between the poems of *commonplace* and those of *only lines,* the reader will find the poems that have appeared in *Five Takes* (1974), a collection that also included works of other poets. We suspect these poems have been quite forgotten, and we hope that their reappearance here will bring back pleasant memories of Arthur's earlier writings. Some of the poems in *Five Takes* reappear in *commonplace*, and we reproduce that repetition here, in order to respect the integrity of each collection. In all, we are happy to present to readers this collection, which, for the first time, gathers Arthur's published poems within a single volume.

Jenny Yap & Irving Goh

ACKNOWLEDGEMENTS

JENNY YAP and IRVING GOH would like to thank Paul Kratoska and Peter Schoppert at National University of Singapore (NUS) Press for their warm reception of and subsequent support for the idea of publishing this collection of poems by Arthur Yap. At NUS Press, gratitude is also due to Christine Chong for her meticulous editorial assistance and management. Most sincere thanks are also extended to Ying-Ying Tan, Miyuki Nagaoka, Rajeev Patke, Ong Sor Fern, Yeow Kai Chai, Boey Kim Cheng, Ho Chee Lick, and Nathalie Handal, all of whom have given help and advice in their own ways in the process of putting together this collection. They also thank the National Arts Council for their support for this collection through the Publication & Translation Grant.

Irving Goh thanks Jenny Yap and Paul Kratoska for the opportunity to write the introduction. He is also grateful to Rajeev Patke for reading versions of it, and for all his comments and suggestions, which helped make it a stronger piece. He also thanks Dominick LaCapra and Timothy Murray for a 2012–13 fellowship at the Society for the Humanities, where he was able to work on the introduction. Appreciation is also extended to Lionel Wee and the Department of English Language and Literature at NUS for providing him office space, which allowed him to work on the final stages of this collection.

CREDITS

Acknowledgement is made to the following publications in which some of the poems have appeared:

Focus, Singapore
Poetry Singapore, Singapore
Poet, India
New Directions, Singapore
Pacific Quarterly, New Zealand
Ariel, Calgary
Singa, Singapore
Solidarity, Philippines
Southeast Asian Review of English, Malaysia
Tenggara, Malaysia
Westerly, Australia
Look East, Bangkok
Tumasek, Singapore
New Voices of the Commonwealth, London
The Flowering Tree, Singapore
The Second Tongue, Singapore
Literature in English, Ontario
Skoob PACIFICA Anthology, London
Anthology of ASEAN Literatures, Singapore
The Oxford Book of Friendship, London
Journeys: Words, Home and Nation, Singapore
the space of city trees, Singapore
AWARENESS, Singapore
Straits Times Life! Book Tabloid, Singapore
Quarterly Literary Review of Singapore, Singapore
Language for a New Century, New York
Writing Singapore, Singapore

REALIA:

A SHORT INTRODUCTION TO THE

POETRY OF ARTHUR YAP

As NOTED IN the Preface, this collection presents, for the first time, all the published poems of Arthur Yap within a single volume. All the poems from his four major collections—*only lines* (1971), *commonplace* (1977), *down the line* (1980), and *man snake apple & other poems* (1986)—are reprinted here.[1] Included as well are the poems collected in *Five Takes* (1974), which he published with four other poets, and the poems written around 2001. With the publication of this collection, close to a decade after his passing, one could ask: how can one bring a new reading to Yap's poems, not only for readers who are already familiar with them but also for those who are reading them for the first time through this present collection? It is by now *commonplace* to say that Yap's poetry touches on "everyday life,"[2] or, in his own words, "ordinary things."[3] But what is it about ordinary things and everyday life that make them interesting poetic material for him? And what can we learn from ordinary things and everyday life when, through his poetry, we look at them again? A response to these questions might offer us a new perspective on Yap's poems, and my response in this short and modest introduction is that it is all a matter of *realia*, especially the *realia* of ordinary things and everyday life.

According to the *Oxford English Dictionary*, the word *realia* comes from postclassical Latin, and was the neuter plural form of *realis*, the meaning of which, as we would say today, is *real* in the adjectival sense. In more contemporary usage, *realia*, as a noun, bears two meanings: 1) real things or actual facts, especially as distinct from theories about or reactions to them; objective or experiential data, and 2) facts, objects, and materials from everyday life used as teaching aids. As will be seen shortly, both the etymology and contemporary meaning of

---

[1] I note here that *commonplace* appears in the lowercase on the title page, while in the case of *down the line*, the title is in the uppercase. I suspect Yap was in general inclined to use the lowercase, not only for the titles of poems but also for the titles of the collections. That preference is rather evident in the later collection of selected poems, *the space of city trees* (2000), where the lowercase is kept for both the cover and title page, not to mention that all the poem titles there are also in lowercases, including those selected from *man snake apple*, where the titles were capitalized in the original collection.

[2] Anne Brewster, Introduction to Arthur Yap's *the space of city trees*, 2000, xi.

[3] Arthur Yap, Interview with Anne Brewster [1996], *Asiatic* 2 (1), 2008, 99.

realia are not foreign to Yap; *realia* is also a word of choice in one of his poems. And if Yap were inclined towards the word *realia*, I believe that he deploys it in contradistinction to *reality*. This is not to say that he takes *realia* to be separate from, or outside of, *reality*. On the contrary, he is well aware that the latter is constituted by *realia*. The problem lies with us, however: we who have refused to acknowledge especially the *realia* of ordinary things in reality, rendering them something other than what they are instead. Hence, as Yap writes in "man snake apple," we have created for ourselves the reality of "organized leisure, civilized swindle, / top-ten everything, mass trances, pop-whatever." Caught up in this constructed reality, we have lost all sense of recognizing or appreciating the *realia* of common objects and occurrences. Or worse, we do not even let them be: we cannot let an abandoned bicycle rest in its disengagement or even freedom from all meaning (as in the poem "location"), and we forget how to see "trees child and rain" "so precisely" as they are (as in the poem "it rains today").

I would argue here that poetry for Yap can help re-familiarize ourselves with the *realia* of ordinary things and everyday life. Anne Brewster has argued that Yap's poetry has an "effect of defamiliarisation," allowing us to see "trees child and rain / so precisely" in the poem "it rains today" only because the poet puts in place "a little shift / either side of reality."[4] I would suggest a more nuanced or critical consideration of that reality, however; for, as suggested above, reality, under Yap's observation, has not much place for the *realia* of "trees child and rain." Reality, and I invoke the poem "man snake apple" again, tends to be deluged by the spectacle of man "perform[ing] marvellous feats" or "creat[ing] patents." This reality, in other words, is where the *realia* of "trees child and rain" have been defamiliarized rather. Poetry can help us recalibrate our perception, or bring about "a little shift / either side of reality," so that we can *re-familiarize* ourselves with how "trees child and rain" are precisely as they are. To reiterate then, poetry according to Yap can help us regain a sense of *realia*, help us relearn how to look at and appreciate the *realia* of ordinary things and everyday life that exist beside the reality that we have created for ourselves.

One way to recognize *realia* again is perhaps to accept the fact of the world in all its senses, that is to say, not only the world as the occurrences of things either as how they are or how they unfold by themselves, but also how things are managed or controlled to appear and develop as such. In the Singapore context, one of the most pronounced manifestations of *realia*

---

[4] Introduction to *the space of city trees*, xii.

understood in this manner inheres in the language spoken by the inhabitants of the city-space. One could even be more precise to say that this *realia* for the Singapore case is constituted by *languages*. The plurality of languages is due to the multiracial and/or multiethnic situation of the country, a situation generated since the nineteenth century when Singapore was a colonial outpost of the United Kingdom. At that time, people from China, India, and the surrounding Southeast Asian countries migrated to Singapore to work and live there, bringing along with them a multiplicity of languages. As far as the short history of Singapore as a postcolonial independent nation goes, the political party in power since the late 1960s has tried, through its education and language policies, especially in the 1980s, to control the evolution of multilingualism in the country, encouraging instead its subjects to rigorously adopt "standard" English.[5] The objective of these policies obviously was for the citizens of the city-space to effectively partake, without communicational hiccups, in the global economy that was dominated then by Anglo-American companies. To that end, these policies were even supplemented by government-sponsored campaigns—and the target was clearly citizens of Chinese heritage—to reduce, if not eradicate, the use of Chinese languages, derogatorily deemed "dialects" in these campaigns, other than Mandarin.[6]

---

[5] In case I give the impression that it is a monolingual language policy that the State promotes, let it be said here that it is in fact a bilingual education policy that the State has put in place. It remains undeniable, however, that the State privileges the mastering of "standard" English, while it is almost indifferent to how its subjects perform in their second language acquisition. For more on the politics or ideology behind language policies in Singapore, see Christopher Stroud and Lionel Wee's "Consuming Identities: Language Planning and Policy in Singaporean Late Modernity" (*Language Policy* 6 (2): 253–79, 2007) and Lionel Wee's "'Burdens' and 'Handicaps' in Singapore's Language Policy: On the Limits of Language Management" (*Language Policy* 9 (2): 97–114, 2010). On my part, I have also tried to elucidate the complex and problematic relation between the State's bilingual education policy and the city-space's multilingual ecology in "Singapore Pharmakon" (*Social Identities* 13 (3): 393–409, 2007) and "The Politics of Language in Contemporary Singapore Cinema" (*Interventions* 13 (4): 610–26, 2011), both co-written with Ying-Ying Tan.

[6] Granted that there is a certain pragmatic, economic necessity for the citizens of this city-space to adopt English as their first language the moment they attend schools, the underlying critique here aims at the State's will to undermine other languages while implementing its pro-English language policies. Here, I also take issue with the State's claim to promote "standard" English. Certainly, for Singapore's citizens to partake in international trade, or to benefit from global economic and educational opportunities, there is a need for them to have a good command of English that is comprehensible to other speakers of English. One could call that variety of English "standard" English, evacuated of grammatical

And yet, the use of language by its speakers, or even language itself, has a way of eliding total control attempted at through policies. In other words, despite the State's endeavors to denigrate or even negate certain languages, users of those languages, should they desire it, will always find avenues to allow the languages to continue to be spoken, and even evolve. This is perhaps especially so with the colloquial form of Singapore English, which is undoubtedly at some distance from "standard" English, given its at times deliberate and at times non-conscious playfulness with the latter's grammar, including introducing from time to time into its idiom the vocabulary and syntax of other languages of this city-space such as Malay or Hokkien.[7] Certainly, colloquial Singapore English in this sense escapes intelligibility for the uninitiated foreigner, and this is the form of Singapore English that the State has tried to circumvent or even eliminate. It seeks to do so because, not trusting its subjects to be able to transpose to the register of "standard" English when it comes to official or formal meetings with foreigners, it is convinced that Singapore English stands as communicational obstacles with respect to successful business deals, and hence sees it as a huge cost to the economic well-being of the nation. Singapore English, however, as said, is a colloquial form of communicational exchange, which means that it is a language common almost to all who have been living in this city-space. That also means that colloquial Singapore English constitutes an undeniable aspect of the *realia* of their everyday existence, which even gives them an immanent sense of belonging to this city-space, a sense that largely escapes all the State's efforts in fabricating a contrived Singaporean identity through the mimicry of a "standard" English.

infelicities or idiosyncratic discourse particles. While that "standard" might appear as a neutral medium for international communication, the notion of "standard" English according to the State in Singapore is not so neutral, not to mention that it lacks a "standard" definition. In the 70s and the 80s, when the United Kingdom was still regarded as the place of prestigious education, the State considered British English as the "standard." When American universities became the force to reckon with from the 1990s onwards, the State began shifting its stance and took American English to be the "standard." In any case, one should nonetheless take a critical stance with regard to the notion of a "standard," in spite of all pragmatic and/ or economic considerations. One should always ask: What makes something a "standard"? Why should one entity be a "standard" and not another? Who determines what is a "standard"? Do we need to have something as "standard"?
[7] I note here that while linguists so far have been working out the origins (e.g., Malay or Hokkien) of the many loan words in Singapore English, they do not seem keen to affirm the playful aspect of Singapore English with regard to both "standard" English and other languages. In my limited ways, I tried to provide a positive account of that playfulness in "Singapore *Pharmakon*".

While the State seeks to simplify, organize, and control the *realia* of language, one could say that for Yap, poetry, on the contrary, must try as best to capture that *realia*: one must allow language—in all its heterogeneous rhythms, acoustics, lexicographies, and interactions with other languages, in everyday usage—to reverberate in poetry without judgment. Yap has demonstrated this poetic skill inimitably in the early "2 mothers in a h d b playground," and has done likewise again in later poems such as "The correctness of flavour" or "wet and dry."[8] in "the correctness of flavour," we have a classic setting of his poetry: no place particularly outstanding (another aspect of *realia*, which I hope will become evident in due course), but a simple or even typical ice cream shop that one commonly finds in a cosmopolitan city such as Singapore. That idiom of colloquial Singapore English is immediately recognizable in the disinterested waitress as she delivers a mechanical reiteration of the day's (un) available flavors to a mother and her child: "lime sherbert today don't have. / mango got. strawberry also don't have." The parent, as intolerant as the State of the common linguistic idiom, decides to rectify things: "today DOESN'T have. / today DOES NOT have." The parent surely comes off as presumptuous with her pedantic revision, to the point of sounding absurd (and perhaps this absurd presumptuousness resounds in the judgmental tone of those who cannot accept the *realia* of language in this city-space). The absurdity becomes more pronounced when we see her child responding in an idiom closer to the colloquial variety than "standard" English—"mango can, anything can. / any anything also can," to which his mother has no rejoinder. One should be fair, however, to say that in terms of accepting the *realia* of language, that is to say, language in both its "standard" and non-"standard" varieties, there is indeed some sort of "impasse" for every interlocutor here: there is not only the refusal of the mother to accept the common idiom of communicational exchange between citizens, but also the refusal of the waitress and the child to accede to the expectations of conducting one's discourse in "standard" English. It is not simply the case therefore that what "hold no truth" are the "immediate *realia*" of available ice cream flavors for the child; it is also the *realia* of the linguistic matrix of this city-space, constituted by the common linguistic idiom, "standard" English, and

---

[8] To be sure, not all of Arthur Yap's poems are inflected by colloquial Singapore English. As Rajeev Patke has noted, he can write with "bookish" (i.e., "standard") English; and Patke continues to say that Arthur Yap "at his best excels at projecting a voice that is uniquely personal, but capable of absorbing Singlish [i.e., colloquial Singapore English] into the dramatization of a wide range of local sensibilities and speech habits" (*Postcolonial Poetry in English*, 74–5).

other languages, which, in ways respective to the points of view of the mother, the child, and the waitress, "hold no truth."

The phrase "immediate *realia*" further points to another aspect of *realia* to which Yap is equally sensitive: the temporal dimension. I have mentioned earlier that Singapore English is a linguistic idiom that is always playfully deviating from the norms of "standard" English and other languages. One could also say that it is constantly evolving, taking on various manifestations at different points in time. Yap is no less aware of such transformations, which explains, as an ear alert to nuances will be able to discern, the different character of Singapore English captured in the later "correctness of flavour" in comparison to the early "2 mothers in a h d b playground." In the eyes (or ears) of many readers, the latter poem might be a representative poem of Yap,[9] since it accurately and poetically captures the entire musicality—the rhythm, acoustics, cadence, and diction—of Singapore English. Yap, however, is keenly attuned to the fact that that musicality belongs to the epoch of the late 70s or the 80s, and that Singapore English in the twenty-first century has quite a different ring to it.[10] He therefore does not let "2 mothers in a h d b playground" remain representative of a poetics of Singapore English. The later poems then stand as an acknowledgement that what is registered in an earlier poem can become dated when one rereads it in more contemporaneous contexts. Poetry according to Yap must always approximate itself as best as possible to the *realia* of language of the present moment. There is nothing for it, if it is to hold on to a past idiom: "there is no future in nostalgia," as he says in a poem of the same title, a poem as well loved by readers as "2 mothers in a h d b playground."[11] And yet, that does not amount to a renunciation of what was written in the past. Rather, what it implies for poetry committed to *realia*—poetry that undertakes

[9] See, for example, the introduction to *Writing Singapore: An Historical Anthology of Singapore Literature*, 175.
[10] I do believe that some of the iterations in "2 mothers in a h d b playground," such as "throwing money / into the jamban [a Malay word for drain] is the same. / ah beng's father spends so much, / takes out the mosaic floor & wants / to make terazzo (*sic*) or what," and "come, cheong, quick go home & bathe. / ah pah wants to take you chya-hong [a Hokkien term meaning "eating air" literally, which parodies the image of driving one's car with the top and windows down] in new motor-car," are hardly used or heard in twenty-first century Singapore.
[11] I acknowledge that "2 mothers in a h d b playground" can be read as a parody or satire of local speech habits, and I am quite certain that many readers who either bear, or are familiar with, those speech patterns are also aware of that satirical dimension of the poem. These same readers embrace the poem nevertheless, holding it in high esteem even, and I believe this is so because, in spite of its satirical possibility, what matters more is that the poem has actualized the

6

the task or even responsibility of inscribing the idioms or speech patters of a language at a particular time, celebrating the value that they have for the speakers of that language at that time—is that it must accept taking the risk of sounding dated at a later time, understanding that supplementary glosses will eventually be needed for future generations of readers to grasp some of its meanings.

To be sensitive to the temporal evolution of language not only means being attentive to the changes in the idioms and the speech patterns that "native" speakers bring to the language, but also being attentive to how the language mutates due to external influences considered fashionable at a certain time. In "Wet and Dry" then, we see on the page a Singapore English inflected with American English, a growing linguistic phenomenon among the younger generation in Singapore since the early twentieth century. A waitress at a sandwich shop asks customers *"doant wanna mayer?"* [(you) don't want mayo(nnaise)?]. This is quickly revealed to be an awkwardly adopted American English accent, its pretentiousness soon betrayed by her articulations of *"huat hui huan?"* [what (do) you want?] and *"why or wry?"* [white or rye], which reveal the irreducible trace of the Chinese language —probably the waitress' household idiom—inflecting her speech pattern. This mutated form of Singapore English, unfortunately, is quite incomprehensible, escaping the understanding not only of foreigners but also, as the poem testifies, of locals likewise: to the question *"doant wanna mayer?"* the poet thought it concerned "a person soon to be rejected;" and to the question *"why or wry?"* the couple was given the impression that sandwiches, "like accustomed noodles, came with a choice / of wet and dry."

Comprehensible or not, ridiculous or not, fashionable or not, "standard" or not, everything that happens to language remains the *realia* of language in this city-space, that is to say, language in its plurality and heterogeneity as traversed by a multiplicity of idioms. *Realia* is quite a mixed bag, therefore; or else, a matter of "mixed shots," as Yap puts it in another later poem of the same title. At the outset, that poem gives us a snapshot of the people that have gathered at Singapore's shopping district, Orchard Road. We have then "groups of housemaids on an evening outing / compared employers, teenagers roller-bladed. / gathered around litter-bins, smokers exhaled / mushroom-puffs," a tourist, and a woman "anxiously awaiting / an unacquainted colleague." On any

aesthetic potentiality of colloquial Singapore English, if not immortalized colloquial Singapore English by giving it poetic form. Such aesthetic affirmation of colloquial Singapore English is in sharp contrast to the State's language policies, through which one learns rather to despise local speech patterns.

other day, this composition would be communitarian only in a loose, random sense, not to mention that there is really not much relation existing between these different groups of people. On this day, however, something serendipitous happens. A passerby mistakes the tourist and the woman for a couple, since the woman "was within range / of the [tourist's camera] lens, but not the focus," and proceeds to take a picture of them, thinking "they were / man and wife and a silly sculpture," while the woman thought the tourist "was that colleague." What takes place then is a chance encounter, a trinity formed by the "samaritan" and two people from different places, "he of taiwan and she of k.l.," passing through Singapore, leading to "a drink"—an ensemble of mixed alcoholic shots perhaps—"at the sidewalk." One should not expect this gathering to be more binding than the other "mixed shots" of housemaids, teenagers, and smokers. This is because, a short while later, "pauses became longer, / the conversation thinner. there being nothing / more plangent, each left the other two." Within a short passage of time then, we witness an aspect of *realia* that concerns a part of our everyday lives whereby we meet people by chance and leave them. The composition of this *realia* is neither preconceived nor fixed, but is indeed more like accidental "mixed shots," taking form on the one hand because of one person's "unnecessary visit," and on the other, because of another person's being "within range / [...] but not [in] focus," all these brought together at "the blinding speed of a shutter," soon after which all parties will disperse.

Given the at times serendipitous or surprising dimension of *realia* as observed in "mixed shots," should one also think of *realia* in terms of an event, especially the event in the philosophical sense? The event is a topic with which late twentieth and early twenty-first century continental philosophy has been preoccupied. The French philosopher Jacques Derrida, for example, has called for the thinking of the event as distinct from the future. According to Derrida, the future is something that can be programmed, and something that one expects to unfold according to that program. Such a future is in contradistinction with an event, since the event, as Derrida puts it, must have the element of surprise: it happens beyond all calculations, which also implies that it might even appear impossible or unthinkable; and yet, when it arrives, one must welcome it in all its surprise or eventfulness.[12] *Realia* in Yap's "mixed shots," which, as noted above, touch on moments in everyday life where occurrences are not only vague but also traversed by unforeseen phenomena, can be said to resonate with

---

[12] For Derrida's discussion on the event, *see Spectres de Marx* (1993) and *Dire l'événement est-ce possible?* (2003).

Derrida's notion of the event in that respect. Besides Derrida, another French philosopher, Alain Badiou, is also invested in the question of the event. The element of the impossible resides in Badiou's event as much as in Derrida's: as Badiou explicates, the event is impossible because the existing status quo regarding the knowledge of things has refused to acknowledge the event's existence and considered it nonexistent instead. In the face of that situation, Badiou then argues that one must bring about a certain forcing [*forçage*] so that the event can see the light of day: one must declare a militant faith in the event, and labor to ensure that conditions are in place to allow the event to unfold as fully as possible. According to Badiou's philosophy, poetry, in its radical experiment with form, can bear the trace of this event; and, as Badiou sees it, Mallarmé's poetry has been exemplary in this respect.[13] Given that Yap's poems such as "2 mothers," "the correctness of flavour," and "wet and dry" give form to poetry intercalated with the colloquial form of Singapore English, something that was considered unworkable or even unacceptable in Singapore until Yap showed how it might be done, one could also say then that his inscription of *realia* in linguistic terms bears the sense of the event according to Badiou.

And yet, one can quickly recall Yap's "there is no future in nostalgia" once again to underscore that his understanding of *realia* takes distance from Badiou's militant fidelity to the event. In Badiou's commitment to seeing the event unfold in actuality, there is a refusal to allow the passage of time to transform or dilute the event, or, put more simply, a refusal to accept the fact that things change over time. With Yap's *realia*, however, one is not so hung up on the event. This is clearly demonstrated in "there is no future in nostalgia," and it will be instructive to quote the short poem in its entirety:

there is no future in nostalgia

& certainly no nostalgia in the future of the past.
now, the corner cigarette-seller is gone, is perhaps dead.
no, definitely dead, he would not otherwise have gone.
he is replaced by a stamp-machine,
the old cook by a pressure-cooker,
the old trishaw-rider's stand by a fire hydrant,
the washer-woman by a spin-dryer

---

[13] Badiou's extensive treatment of the event is in his two-volume magnum opus *Être et événement* (1988; 2006).

> & it goes on
> in various variations and permutations.
> there is no future in nostalgia.

The sense of "future" here is very close to that which Derrida critiques. It is not something that arrives in its absolute surprise, previously unanticipated or unexpected. Rather, it is the past, "in [its] various variations and permutations." Even then, it "goes on," which means it does not look back. There "certainly [is] no nostalgia in the future of the past," and on this point, one can say that there is clearly no Badiouian fidelity to the event in Yap's poetry. For Yap, to hold on to the past per se, that is to say, to dwell in nostalgia, one will be hard-pressed to move on; or worse, there will simply be "no future." Of course, it is not always a good thing if things change only in the name of so-called "progress," especially technological progress, where the traces of human spirit and human endeavor are rapidly erased indifferently.[14] The overt willingness to accept the inevitability of change in "there is no future in nostalgia" is therefore counterbalanced by a detectable sense of regret for the negative consequences of such cold, mechanical processes. That regret is expressed through the inscription of the corner cigarette-seller, the old cook, the old trishaw-rider, and the washer-woman—figures that have rapidly disappeared along the way of Singapore's hyper-modernization. While there is undoubtedly an archival effect in the poetic inscription of these figures, which serves to remind us what we have lost in human terms in our pursuit of "progress," one should note that it is done without insisting on any return to these figures of history. That is perhaps poetry's way of accepting the fact of the world's incessant "progress", while offering a critique of that "progress" at the same time, which surely is in contrast to attitudes that try to keep pace with change in uncritical ways—an undeniable aspect of *realia* reflected in "i think (a book of changes)," where a shopkeeper, when asked about the demand "to time in with the changes," such as changing shop names, can only respond: "what? / "what do i think of it?"

In witnessing the passing or "progress" of the world, one could also say that a poetics of *realia* does not make an event out of things, or one does not mark something out as a spectacular exception above other things, which would imply a denigration of the latter as merely quotidian or insignificant

---

[14] My placing of "progress" in quotation marks is a nod to Walter Benjamin's work that critiques the late nineteenth-century to early twentieth-century shift towards an age of mechanical reproducibility.

in comparison. In Yap's poetry therefore, there are, in respect of every event that arrives, no exceptional events: one event is as eventful as another, even though it might be regarded as a non-event. That is to say, the non-event is also an event in his poetics of *realia*. Or, his poetics does not make an event of an event, elevating it above other events—not even the fall of man. In Yap's poetic reconstruction of the Genesis story in "man snake apple," the fall of man befalls with "a minimum of event," and it occurs not on a remarkable day but "day seven," which is incidentally the uneventful day of rest in God's creation of the world according to Genesis. It is something of "a minimum of event" because, in Yap's poetic discernment, it is not something that has been unique to that day "from anytime." Instead, "it was forever & forever & forever," and "it begins again today." And if the fall of man is something that "was forever & forever & forever," it is then, at the end of it all, rather quotidian; and, as Yap tells us in "commonplace," one "should never whip the commonplace / for the meaning of its opposite."

In a way, the fall of man is as much an event as the aunt's wedding attended by a little girl in the poem aptly named "event." As the poet observes, there is in fact nothing extraordinary about things and people at the wedding. The little girl is as much "combed and frilled" as the bridal bouquet. The bride, on her part, "combed & frail, / smile smaller [than the little girl's]," with her "teeth stuck to her gums," actually paints a less than pleasant picture, except "the occasion gave it beauty." "Eventually," the little girl, when all grown up, will repeat her aunt's wedding ritual: as a bride, her hands will be gloved similarly like "2 gloved mice"; the typical dish for Chinese weddings in the 1980s, "peking ducks," will be served; and the bride of the poem "will be / at the little girl's wedding." Given that the wedding ritual will repeat itself again, or that the fall of man is "forever & forever & forever," one should not, however, presume that the repetitions are without differences. I quote from "commonplace" again: "everything has happened before / but there is nothing to compare it / each time, with each time that it recurs." In other words, should an event repeat itself, one should be attentive to the nuances that occur each time, sensitive to the differences that make each occurrence different from the one before or after. Otherwise, and I borrow Yap's words from "fair youth," "the analogous looks / of one [would] seem to nullify those of the others." But the point here, again, is not to privilege one event over another, or to highlight one moment of the event above the rest: grasping *realia* would mean, one could say, adopting a more democratic perspective on events, never imposing any hierarchy on them.

In order to acknowledge that there are always events, rather than a singular event, a poetics of *realia* perhaps must also be willing to let things pass, to let things devolve across time, and refrain from resisting all the changes and transformation brought about by time. One has to accept, as Yap writes in the poem "location," that "some things remain / some things pass, / some things are tired." In a move that prefigures "there is no future in nostalgia," he will also write, "do not change the day / to bring in yesterday." He continues: "if you see a bicycle / leaning on the grass / neither tired nor cleaned / then it is just resting / sufficiently / to make no sense at all." This is not to say that one adopts a passive position before the unfolding of *realia*. As suggested above in the discussion of "there is no future in nostalgia," poetry can have a critical function in the face of a highly accelerated technological "progress" that tends to efface all traces of the human. Poetry can challenge that forced oblivion by reinscribing the human trace into the poetic landscape or poetic history of a given site. In other words, poetry can always actively rupture the speed and trajectory of "progress" by recording events that get passed over, giving place to a time of reading where we can take stock of them. This is perhaps the lesson of "still-life v," a lesson on how to look at a common site such as a park and its common feature such as the pond:

> where does this park end & begin again?
> do not be misled by the park. it begins & ends
> every morning; its attendants arriving,
> its lovers departing.
> where does this pond end & its bank begin?
> it begins in a moist susurrus of ripples
> & doesn't ever end, even at the edge
> of its beginning where wild watercress grows.
> nothing is happening,
> a non-event at no time recorded for posterity.
> yet, there's a still pond wants to be fed,
> a pond wherever it outlines.
> & it doesn't especially want anything to happen
> except it's a sunny day
> with watercress soughing at its side.

One could say that events—especially non-events such as the flow of a pond or the "event" of a non-extraordinary wedding of an anonymous woman, events so commonplace that they seem to recur in "various variations and permutations"—want to be written about. As Yap writes in the early poem "only lines," "you need lines / to add up this same old story." But again, except for them to be written, these (non-)events do not "want anything to happen": they do not demand physical intervention in their development, mutation, and degradation. The devolution of (non-)events, in their growth and decay, to reiterate, is but the *realia* of the world in its passage over time. One witnesses it in its passing, and one can record it, after which one has to let go and move on, "before," as Yap says in the poem "i am not sure," "the tentative becomes conditional." Put another way, one must always leave *realia* in their "mixed shots" of events, of things expected and unexpected; one must leave them in their uncertainty perhaps, unsure as to where they begin and end. To stay too long with any of these events, or to be fixated by them, and consequently to fixate them too, is to render what has passed as something "conditional," which conditions or determines what is to come in the future. In that case, we will have a future that Derrida denounces, in other words, a future without events that arrive in their complete surprise, without events that are never expected in advance. According to Yap in "down the line," there will be nothing much to be written then: "any event, being given, / predetermined, is at the outset already silent."

Having said that poetry can capture the passing of *realia*, or more precisely—and this is said in complete awareness of its paradoxical import since *realia* are never precise—traces of *realia* in passing, one must not henceforth think that poetry has the last word on them. At times, words move too fast, moving ahead even before any part of *realia* is a reality. Yap was well aware of this: in "in the quiet of the night," he writes, "words will move on more swiftly / than tomorrow will be now," indeed to the point where "tomorrow morning," as he observes in "dialogue," "now it is." In this case, one gets ahead of *realia*, barely grasping them. At other times, words fall almost completely short. This is the case with regard to friendship, as the poem "your goodness" acknowledges: "the poem / is short, inadequate &, except for a word, / totally redundant." In recognizing the inadequacy or overzealous excess of words or even poetry, Yap seems to suggest that poetry must not be complacent to think that it is able to capture or come up with an adequate representation of *realia*. That, for him, would perhaps only mark the failure of poetry, a failure arising from our hubristic ingenuity "of stilling words" as he says in the poem "words." In the poem "scroll painting," that failure is compared to what a painting presents: "here is transient beauty / caught in permanence / but of what avail is such perpetual unattainment? / i know the stupid bird can never eat the stupid peach."

Rather than dwelling in the world of words or poetry, we must always keep in mind, as Yap does in "12-times table," that at least two worlds are at play at the time of writing: the "depicting" world in which the poet is caught up, and the physical world out there, which is always "transmogrifying beyond" all present manifestations. This reminder serves to instruct us that poetry, at best, is but a passage back to *realia*, a way to remind us that we are always in their midst, always amidst the "mixed shots" of everyday events inflected with the heterogeneity of everyday speech. There are *realia* before poetry; and there are other, different ones after poetry. Poetry then, for Yap, is a means to underscore our being-in-*realia*, and to make us realize once again what *realia* can teach us beyond the instruction of institutional knowledge or even of poetry. If "the distant orange sun taught different greens," as Yap notes in "cianjur," it is not poetry but *realia* that make it so.

Irving Goh
Society for the Humanities, Cornell University
Paris-Ithaca/New York, 2013

Works Consulted

Brewster, Anne. "Interview with Arthur Yap." *Asiatic* 2 (1): 97–108, 2008.

Chung, Yee Chong, Sng Boh Khim, Arthur Yap, Yeo Bock Cheng, and Robert Yeo. *Five Takes: Poems by Chung Yee Chong, Sng Boh Khim, Arthur Yap, Yeo Bock Cheng, and Robert Yeo*. Singapore: University of Singapore Society, 1974.

Patke, Rajeev S. *Postcolonial Poetry in English*. Oxford: Oxford University Press, 2006.

Poon, Angelia, Philip Holden, and Shirley Geok-lin Lim, ed. *Writing Singapore: An Historical Anthology of Singapore Literature*. Singapore: National University of Singapore Press, 2009.

Yap, Arthur. *commonplace*. Singapore, Kuala Lumpur and Hong Kong: Heinemann, 1977.

———. *down the line.* Singapore, Kuala Lumpur and Hong Kong: Heinemann, 1980.

———. *man snake apple & other poems*. Singapore: Heinemann, 1986.

———. *only lines*. Kuala Lumpur: Federal Publications, 1971.

———. *the space of city trees: selected poems*. With an Introduction by Anne Brewster. London: Skoob, 2000.

mixed shots

groups of housemaids on an evening outing
compared employers, teenagers roller-bladed.
gathered around litter-bins, smokers exhaled
mushroom-puffs. in the energy of orchard road,
a tourist giraffed his neck to take a picture
of a sculpture fronting a mall —
a necessary souvenir of his unnecessary visit.

standing near, a woman, anxiously awaiting
an unacquainted colleague, was within range
of the man's lens, but not the focus.

soon as he had clicked, a tap on the shoulder.
a passer-by: want me to take a picture of you both?

baffled, his camera taken; led to where
the woman was. at the same time, she,
thinking he was that colleague, stepped forward.
to the samaritan's call, the man turned round;
then both froze and smiled.

the passer-by had thought they were
man and wife and a silly sculpture.

embarrassed laughter, a drink at the sidewalk.
they chatted – he of taiwan and she of k.l.,
here on a conference. then, pauses became longer,
the conversation thinner. there being nothing
more plangent, each left the other two.

the samaritan to further deeds;
the man back to photographing another souvenir
without fetching up another instant wife;
and, she, back in her hotel, was amazed
that marriage was the blinding speed of a shutter.

on offal

lau lim pored over a stack of brochures –
sanyo, hitachi, national, westinghouse.
a washing machine, a compact dummy-thing,
has replaced the dhobi, spreading out clothes to dry.

this man, as job epithets go,
is in the porcine line – stall 27;
his pig-intestine soup diffuses aroma to all.

a pig is a very compact arrangement
and lends itself to gastronomic deconstruction,
every which part is tedious and messy
but no parts more so than the innards –
slippery, slithery ropes to hang
culinary excellence on.

the scraping of the mucilage takes two people
some hours each early morning, a job
of moan and groan. worst of all,
not showing up is total loss of trade to the man
pursuing the brochures with a vengeance.

bypassing light cotton, delicate fabrics,
and other settings, his two sonys whirl and churn
loud and clear. if you look at the glass windows,
grey snakes glide in quick-heavy motion.
and, from the bowels of these machines
to the boiling cauldron, it is a duplicitous movement.

what a congruence
of processes it all is:
the soup arrives,
for you and for you,
steaming in your face.

fair youth

they are handsome. perhaps had there been
a different set of good looks in any of them,
s/he would have stood out. the analogous looks
of one seem to nullify those of the others:
the beauty of flowers, the distinctive marks
of one, faithfully duplicated in the others,
are mutual-cancelling.

they go to the beach each day with water bottles
from which they seem to be weaning
in an everlasting stream. they have their mores
and, these, like traffic lights, are obeyed.
they go to discos and dance the floor away.
always cheerful, the sun doesn't set in their face,
nor does the dark dim the glow of tanned skin.

never peccant, they live the day.
when one broke a leg, the others didn't fuss.
he hobble-crutched alongside. another,
after a motor-bike accident, was named horrors,
a variation of his own.
youth, comfortable with itself, is.

then, one grew quiet and taciturn. a pallor
creamed his tan. the others swam the brilliant
afternoon to a fatigue. on the sand, the loner averred in anguish:
i have AIDS.

life, upside down –
a schedule was set up
and help was everyone
in singular intent to mitigate.
sometimes unsure, sometimes salving;
someone erred, someone saving.
all the time, unwavering.

youth can be, wondrously, fair.

sociability

she used to be a social escort.
after her expiry date, she became
an acupuncturist with a homely mien
not previously maintained in her job.

when her parents got married,
she was four. born on february 29,
she had a real birthday every four years.
no earlier or later proxy-date would do;
not that anyone did anything, leaving her
and her birthday alone for herself·

it was on such a day that she stuck a needle
sharp in a kneecap. the old lady didn't dare
gainsay that an acupuncturist with a homely mien
wouldn't show such avidity as practician.
she stratified her lips into a pencil line.

such was her mood when, alone again,
a tapestry of feelings a single thread
couldn't unravel, she entered the door
of her used-to agency. greeted tepidly,
she accepted her estrangement as she had
her birthday — every one of every three years
was an eked-out shrift.

i won't know what to do now
if i have to go out with total strangers,
my loneliness keeps me company.
tittering inwardly, a former fellow-escort:
it can't be so bad. have a good day.

or night. nights can be that bad
enough to wonder – which highrise,
what floor, mrt track at which point,
until sleep takes over each and every choice
and these potentials, too, are in repose.

CARPE DIEM

the three men at the smith street fish stall
were not there to trade points on pisciculture.
those manning it, framed by large glass tanks
full of freshwater carp and eruptions of bubbles,
nodded at the request for eighty carp :
to be packed in covered polystyrene boxes,
collected at 8 am saturday, and a downpayment,
of course, now.

a birthday present for the patriach :
the three men's father and father-in-law,
seventy-nine years sanctified, had requested
for the carp, not to be feated on,
nor any resturant extravance either,
to be released into three reservoirs :
seletar, peirce, macritchie.

carpe diem. seize the day for the patriach.
his offer of thanks : deo optimo maximo :
a measure of grace. son-in-law, their bellwether,
repeated time and date and places.

nods of the head, everybody's saturday.
the variously released batches of fish flipped
their brilliant tails and never looked back.
it is my conjecture that they didn't;
i wasn't there at the witnessing.

in three batches, neat and sequential :
the beatific stages of the patriach's life?
who am i not partisan to this point?

Arthur Yap
April 2000

VIGNETTES

2001

the correctness of flavour

waiting for the lime sherbert to arrive
mother turned around to her vacuous child:
boy, you heard what i said earlier?
Nowadays, they emphasise english.

boy rolled his squinty eyes to the ceiling.
waitress returned, flustered, and started
on her own emphases:
lime sherbert today don't have.
mango got. strawberry also don't have.

mother, upset and acutely strident:
today DOESN'T have
today DOES NOT have.

boy, beyond any mitigation of flavour:
mango can, anything can.
any anything also can.

the glass of the shop amber-tinted;
boy, facing a tall window, looked malarial
mango and, it being a sunny day,
didn't help the spectrum of quiet light.
strawberry-faced waitress went on mouthing
and serving. mother glared and glowered
over whatever else needed emphasised.
courtesy — nowadays, they emphasise courtesy.
eat healthy — nowadays, they emphasise it healthy.

so mother continued to be trenchant,
boy's squint refused to concede acceptance —
an impasse in an icecream cafe
in which one would endure no let-up
and the other for which immediate realia
hold no truth.

First published in Life! *The Straits Times*, February 12, 2001.

pomegranate

pomegranate, don't drop till i come back,
the child said. behind the wire-mesh fence,
the corner garden in a row of terrace houses
opens itself to the sun a fraction a day.
the year before, the tensile branches on the left
bore three fruit that dropped, little green bulbs.

may's parents then moved across the estate.
the new house: postage-stamp back garden.
two grass ribbons flank the sides, the tiled front
holds two cars, a large his and a smaller hers.

come on, grow. come on, grow, the child bending
over the pomegranate cajoled. grow and grow,
when i come back, you'll be as big as my head.

unwatered, there was rain. unspoken to, the faint
rumble of traffic was a voice. once in a while,
a breeze combed the shard leaves in leaden rhythm.
may thought little more of it, no more than dinner
eaten, homework done.

another child in the old house zipped about,
marked out a vantage point for video viewing;
bored and not a little tired, externalised
in the garden. the cajoled pomegranate,
a happenstance, so big, so lush, arched the branch
to the grass. a split ran all the way down
the epicarp to the calyx lobes, the pulp
showing through the crack bright red and scorched.

how stupid, how stupid, the child said.

First published in Life! *The Straits Times*, February 12, 2001.

this boy's zoo

the boy, on his first visit to the zoo,
is taken totally aback during his stroll.

this is surely a virtual affirmation,
a repetition of what's in the primers:

f for flamingo
g for giraffe
h for hippopotamus
o for orang utan

i've gone through all this:
i've seen all these.

the hippo's too chunky and leatherily abstract,
it can be told by a waft of green stench at your face.
the giraffe doesn't impress with its long-winded neck;
rather, its crinkled ears, no-tech phones, compel.

he notices not how human the orang utans are
but how proximate-simian is his father
and, though his arms don't touch the ground,
they are the long arms of push and pull.
his gestures to them are not reciprocated;
they just sit there, stare and stare and stare,
stroking their chins in ersatz confucianism.

the flamingo's pink is less acerbic than his mother's
pink skirt. as she makes a half-pink turn
and offers a tidbit, the bird sidles away with grace
leaving her arm a short stiff bamboo stick.

some things are not in those primers.

the boy thinks the zoo is a better home.
animals don't piss in lifts, anywhere
is good enough site, and there are no groups
going up and down; no filipino maids to defenestrate.

the giraffe can slide food down its chute,
the hippo has an outsized outdoor bathtub,
the flamingo a pool to cool its metres of legs.
the orang utans breakfast with human guests.

they never tell us all this,
these fixated primers.
the boy thinks he should like
to bone up on evolution,
alternately, be a highrise votary.

First published in Life! *The Straits Times*, February 12, 2001.

wet or dry

a plastic signboard under the logo:
Freshly-Made Sandwiches — All Kinds
i thought it would have been fine had the 's'
dropped off from 'Kinds' — a wholesome meal
kind to stomach, pocket, happily-served.

a small queue ahead; the lone waitress,
as server and cashier, took whatever order
with haughter, not exactly speaking in tongues
or any specific one, hers was trippingly awry.

doant wanna mayer? took me a while
to realize it wasn't a person soon to be rejected.
then, other such labyrinthics:

the teenage couple ahead wondered to each other
about pastrami, and was rosemary chicken
a girl's pet come to this. their turn.
Stepping up, greeted with *huat hui huan?*
or, so it sounded; even my weak ear caught
the oddity and sharp impatience.

a quick rattling of 'All Kinds' helped
in takeaway decision-making.
something chosen,
the filling, not the bread, and this brought:
why or *wry?* i perked up at what sounded
like quick-hash esoterica.

then, glancing at another signboard:
      Bread — Choice of White or Rye
          Plain or Toasted

the couple, now nonplussed, thought aloud
with a sense of incredulity that sandwiches,
like accustomed noodles, came with a choice
of wet or dry.

coward, i broke queue. on such a day,
i couldn't handle my daily bread
which might also be:
wile or rice
while or rise
Y or ..

First published in Life! *The Straits Times*, April 9, 2001.

carpe diem

the three men at the smith street fish stall
were not there to trade points on pisciculture.
those manning it, framed by large glass tanks
full of freshwater carp and eruptions of bubbles,
nodded at the request for eighty carp:
to be packed in covered polystyrene boxes,
collected at 8 am saturday, and a downpayment,
of course, now.

a birthday present for the patriarch:
the three men's father and father-in-law,
seventy-nine years sanctified, had requested
for the carp, not to be feasted on,
nor any restaurant extravagance either,
to be released into three reservoirs:
seletar, pierce, macritchie.

carpe diem. seize the day for the patriarch.
his offer of thanks: *deo optimo maximo*:
a measure of grace. son-in-law, their bellwether,
repeated time and date and places.

nods of the head, everybody's saturday.
the variously released batches of fish flipped
their brilliant tails and never looked back.
it is my conjecture that they didn't;
i wasn't there at the witnessing.

in three batches, neat and sequential:
the beatific stages of the patriarch's life?
who am i not partisan to this point?

First published in Life! *The Straits Times*, April 9, 2001.

laughter

I like the fact that listen is an anagram of silent.
                            — Alfred Brendl

effulgent waves of laughter in the dim hall.
choking back anger, kind to stifled laughter,
the pianist recalled the occasion when, to laugh
away tedium, he heaven-stormed the silence
in the hall. only a handful sat, to be out
of pouring rain. he played fast and loud,
oblivious to the composers' texts.

another free recital this time. no one paid
to listen and few did. more recitals, more silences.
then, at one, the pianist, the true pianist in him
stepped out of himself, sat incognito
with the audience and cringed, the absurdity of it,
the notes sank before currenting air.
himself, now, the laugher.

at one time, all laurels were there —
laudatory reviews, serial bookings.
he used to be such a virtuoso. what a pity,
they said, no one quite knew why.

his performance has not, surprisingly, developed.

he knew why. listen. a bottle, two, a day
didn't help. some composers were also sots
but they wrote and didn't have to play.

VIGNETTES

then something happened, and i really love this:
he took to drinking five bottles a day,
five empty bottles he lifted to his lips,
tilted back his head and imbibed trapped air.
silence.

his performance has, not surprisingly, developed.

First published in Life! *The Straits Times*, April 9, 2001.

33

in search

he came from a broken home.
his parents are separated, over a year now,
i think. and, catching her startled look
he quickly added: both wanted him,
fought hard over him, then neither did
and could hardly wait to get away.

the flat is too small. small flats
make miserable pets.

any excuse, you know, just to get away.
do you want him?

the dog, in one prance, cleared the enclosure,
stopped at her feet, gnawed at her shoe.

i've never had a dog before. i'm not sure
i can handle it. What do you feed it on?

what? no, perhaps not a dog if you don't
want something totally people-oriented.
get a cat.

a cat was hard to get. at pet shops,
the pedigreed exuded such disdain she felt spooked.
little strays, lurking round corners
and bins, belonged there. don't come anywhere
near me, please.

for the nonce, she bought a bvlgari watch
for no reason at all.

hamsters, parrots and, for a change,
some wet things — goldfish, koi, turtles,

but even a translucent seahorse wouldn't do.
glossy posters of pets wouldn't at all.
burlap cats, teak dogs, paper owls didn't.

what to do?

in the search for that pet one searches
for oneself in another guise, whatever traits
in mirror-image empathy.
one is one's own existential pet —
a barracuda, a gnu, a tarzan's mate.

or seek an alternative:
read the appropriate entries in a thesaurus —
animals, pets, companions.
follow the nose. and assume.

First published in Life! *The Straits Times*, June 11, 2001.

shao ti

You can make a fresh start with your last breath.
— Bertolt Brecht

shao ti, little brother, the name chimes
variously: shao ti ti, ti ti, ah tee.
shao ti has many aliases and little else,
his plurality of names spells ostracism.
shao ti, fifty-five, too old to repair,
too young to have chalked up longevity.

who is shao ti, then?

once, a fat baby gift-wrapped in bedding,
a rubber teat in mouth like a kitchen sink.
growing up, losing weight, putting it on again:
fat slim, fat slim,
life was a dietary trochee.
shao ti was a pear with no waistline.
his silhouette, now, has neither youth
nor age, merely a shape.

shao ti sold lottery tickets. some tout
moved into his turf and out, on dimpled elbows,
he landed on another trade, hawking socks.

then shao ti made a mistake.
some are given two, others many more,
margins of error, but his one was all:
the killcrow, his mother-in-law,
a powerhouse familial breaker —
shao ti, in blind fury, flashed a chopper.
the mother-in-law was heard no more.
a quieter street saw him get in a car,
a white one with a red siren.

shao ti, seven years' worth of temporary insanity,
eases his weariness onto a concrete seat.
people's park is hospitable to all
in its unconcern. shao ti reads the papers
or, not at all in any hurry, joins the homeless
who have homes that dehouse them into the streets.

shao ti has known it all —
once swathed in clouds of blue cotton,
it is now middle passage:
some empyrean outset
and an unforetold future that any communal
gestalt could foster but not adumbrate.

First published in Life! *The Straits Times*, June 11, 2001.

brocade

high street, once a plethora of fabric shops
with rustling silks and lustrous brocades:
it was in one of them a wily young woman
settled score with her two sisters-in-law

she lived on private tuition, a misnomer,
conducted noisily to a group of nine
in a little alcove by the front entrance.
her earnings each month, measured out
in that shop, was about a decent length
of the best red brocade. not for herself.
brocade on her would hang like arras
on a chicken-wire mannequin.

her sisters-in-law were not overly harsh
a scolding now and then; but the words cut
to the quick and made her even more abject
about her public tuition. the sisters,
not on friendly terms — one in katong,
the other ensconced in keong saik road.

her future in her hands, she cut the rich fabric
into two, each half ample for a long gown.
not for her. a long gown needed stature.
parcelling each in crepe paper, she took
a long bus ride to katong; then, later,
another to the other's.

a month later, at a niece's wedding —
the bride glowing in white, the pretty chubby
maids in white, a beautiful pastel setting,
pale bright flowers, pale guests —

the two sisters came face to face
and turned the richest maroon,
hairline to floor.

First published in Life! *The Straits Times*, June 11, 2001.

MAN SNAKE APPLE

& OTHER POEMS

Arthur Yap

MAN SNAKE APPLE
1986

tropical paradise

the feel of things. textures. the elastic skin,
gently pliant to the touch. the cold metallic shock
of water in a shaded pool, galvanizing all the pores:

paradise:

staminate & pistillate, they all dance to the thrall of
primeval rhythms. things, things growing so fast; feel the
heat of their regeneration. the friction of leaf against leaf,
bud & bee, pod to pod. among the green mysteries of
certainty, they consume the decay of aged life:

paradise:

at sunrise, a stone falling endlessly
& in it the silence of before & after.
in the silence of before & after, a new stone
falls endlessly &, before it is done,

a head falling.
o lord, it is to you it falls.

jungle, a tall tree falling eternally.
& in it the rapidizing of leaves, stirred birds.
in the timelessness before & after, a new tree
falls within the fallen. being done,

a limb falling.
o lord, it is to you it dies.

stained glass

stained glass
was awesome silence,
was such quiet it indicated paraphrases everywhere.
the branches outside were your fingers
held in benediction.

god was such stillness,
his stained-glass figures stretched
neither forward nor backward in himself.

& at this ruby-amber corner
i could only gaze & piece together
whatever i had want of. i was free
because i was free from myself;
a mere witness in whom arose a great need,
urging like silent desperation, prayer,
to be included. i could be a mote, kill glass,
a sunsteeped blob of blood. a nothingness.

god, such stillness was.
your fingers were there.
what do you hold up to bless?

still-life i

if she sits out in the garden, she's a pile of leaves
with a face. sunk in an armchair, it has an extra pair
of arms, gaunt. day in, day out, she's an arrangement
with different settings. a crab near the kitchen table,
a photograph of a head above a brown dress.

she will not move.

her hands & feet twist like vine, against her heart,
against its wish to be drawn apart.
why did you come into this world?
to pay back all my debts.

turning around in quietness, she lets a rasp
slip across the back of her paper hand.
new day, old familiar ache. it never reneges
into oblivion; always there, its intensity
spans a dull throb to the stab that amazes the flesh.

brooding silence filled with enigma & wonder;
nothing to threaten her now, this pile of leaves.
nothing to threaten now,
nothing to threaten now.

still-life ii

i scribble copious notes
while you mime filtered-down priorities
& not for a moment do i believe you.
yet i do.

caught between a yawn, another ensuing;
caught between glances at raindrops
bouncing semicircularities off the ledge,
i think everything's comical,
as comical as anything that isn't
in this arrangement:

this rite of writing
which doesn't provide an option
to any other kind of mindedness.

it is very clear
this scribble has no ambiguity
because you haven't.

still-life iii

burying one's toes in fine sand
isn't particularly remarkable.
what is is hitting a tiny airpocket,
the sudden vacancy of a little crab
& its departing pincer-jab.

no, even that isn't remarkable.
what is, i am so seldom here,
is i can be here. otherwise,
my toes belong to my shoes.
otherwise, i belong fully to myself.
yet today isn't a rarity i intend to have
absolutely.

still-life iv

the friends' conversation still ranges
across the past as it spreads still
around the table. they ask questions,
not probing into one another's lives.
they would not care to admit what they cannot.
the children are held in the present,
staring over plates & cups. they have no demands
to make of anyone. they have nothing to remember
or to forget. they know exactly what is, isn't,
going to happen next. they cup their faces,
lovely, without a cause to decorate.

still-life v

where does rigour end & rigor mortis begin?
so slender is the distinction, & practice
ensures the perfection of numbing the sensibilities.

where does this counter end & the library begin?
faces looking out of spines to say: look,
this is me & me only. you are my sensibilities
& i wear your heart, your eyes, in my footnotes.

where does this park end & begin again?
do not be misled by the park. it begins & ends
every morning; its attendants arriving,
its lovers departing.
where does this pond end & its bank begin?
it begins in a moist susurrus of ripples
& doesn't ever end, even at the edge
of its beginning where wild watercress grows.
nothing is happening,
a non-event at no time recorded for posterity.
yet, there's a still pond wants to be fed,
a pond wherever it outlines.
& it doesn't especially want anything to happen
except it's a sunny day
with watercress soughing at its side.

still-life vi

something wonderfully familiar about the old lady
selling her jade bracelet; the old goldsmith
in the courtyard dallying with the pretty serving maid.
the old sage, intent upon his pagan loves,
his adoration of god, nevertheless saw every moment
of these sad allegories of human folly:
the gambler's ruin, the libertine's.
how this tripling composite picture would be swept aside.
& how out of this meaninglessness would come order.
orderlies to clean the courtyard,
polish the bracelet, spin loves & bring again
something wonderfully familiar: the old lady
selling her jade bracelet, the old gentleman
dallying with the old lady, the serving maid
with her bracelet & her sage.

still-life vii

a house, i know, is but a temporary abode
but how satisfying to find one which harmonizes:
curtain ears close to the ground,
the forehead slopes towards glasspanes
& holds up a nose, a plant in a beige pot
spreading little moist sibilances in the rain.

two big arms run a path in the garden,
draw up sparrows, dun squirrels, still as stone
near columns of grass, green as spring tea.

the rain the shower, the sun a hot towel.
the tiled pate on top knows all, holds all
to an entire point.

man snake apple

ages the apple slept on the tree
dreaming of stars & storing the distillation
of a thousand storms, outlasted cheiroterous ravages
& survived more golden-red if the moons also blessed.
the snake jounced up & down the tree,
investigated the apple from all round angles,
a circumoral need. but it had no need to feed.
the apple had no meaning. man was trying out
& being tried out by his circumstance.
apple snake man were one, two, three.
the snake could rise & walk over man, the apple
of the circumambient eye. man could walk
slither-poised, hang on branches like a growth.

this was day one,
the first day from anytime.

& all days were easy. all ways led to the way
of the lie. it was the dry season, it was the monsoon,
& what should the land produce? young, the lie of the
            land
produced prodigiously, floriferously;
dazzling, giddying itself. man looked at everything
with the calm of unknowing eyes & did not want.
he remained empty till he did; the lie outright.
the apple lay absolute on the tree, the snake near.
man was somewhere between apple & snake.
he could no longer fly; his wings were lain still

this day,
day two

of whatever calendar wasn't.
butterflies flew with the snake that changed
more swiftly than a spectrum of rainbows on short-loan
& the apple effloresced into protoneons; red, gold,

purple, a runnel of liquids & fugitives, visions.
man looked & felt the first flash of the pain of beauty.
The apple stirred in his heart, its stalk a tuning fork
regulating the earth, orchestrating symphonies of
   mountains,
suzerain dragons that immolated in hauteur.
the sun shone relentlessly white, clarifying the land
like fool's gold. & man performed marvellous feats.
trees grew from his fingers, his ears cornucopias.
but the lie was lain & the splendour could only go on
increasing, increasing, increasing with compound vigour.

(come off it.) onto day three, still increasing.
the fantasy was necessary feed for its own fodder.
there was still no other need
man snake apple
on day four, a day of lull,
a day of unearned blessedness;
the long rays of the sun
dripping like arrows of candlewax,
as small mercies, small-time alarms.

they disappeared on day five
because day five was day five
& all prior pluses & minuses
were not cued this day,
not gathered, not resown, not wanted.

& without the fore-days' diurnal dovetailings,
the day gathered itself as a flower before nightfall,
sufficient for its own context of being, untroubled
by vanity, anxiety or effort, or even happiness.

day six began with a short lineal history
of ancestral promptings & urgings,
a surfeit of wide-awake dreams, of ersatz violence.
it was a weight-lifter who couldn't get the weight up.

from morning to noon, from noon to dusk,
storing upon itself, conserving to have itself reborn.
an umbilication of comatose inertia. the finagling snake
quiet as coiled repose. the voluptuous apple slept on,
heavy as a stone, a minuscule pumpkin.
& ruminative man, poised as his own shily shadow;
an indefinable, incalculable weight on his shoulders.
the apple in his head slow-rattling, a feral football;
the snake in his heart undulating in lazy loops.

day six died.
the world grew young & day seven happened;
a minimum of event, fanfare, cheer-leading.
sun, moon, stars were freshly reordered.
man snake apple multiplied; in endless succession,
the progeny. men killed snakes, ate apples.
apples, detached from trees, dropped on men
& germinated ideas, created patents,
became the targets of crossbows.
snakes bit into serum & have carried it ever since;
popped out of watering holes, appeared in circuses,
slid over tarmac lanes, were run over by cars.

man snake apple were no longer one, two, three.
a fused combination, the progeny in infinite
            permutations.
mensnakesapples built cities, flew as they once did,
fought wars, archiving them as later documentaries,
invented organized leisure, civilized swindle,
top-ten everything, mass trances, pop-whatever.

it was forever & forever & forever

& a day,
today. it begins again today.

your goodness
for Keith

your goodness, i sometimes light
my anger with, is what you have. no one
can burn it away; it is not for my discussion.
i know, near you, i myself feel good.
& this is enough for me, my friend.

this is a life-time friendship; the poem
is short, inadequate &, except for a word,
totally redundant.

dialogue

unused to central london late on a sunday,
how brightly lit the shopfronts are
& how entirely dark the office windows above.
the place looks dead & alive at the same time.

from here to sloane gardens: out of the station,
i'm not sure whether to turn left or right
& this must be the many of many times.
but i'm here. you are at the door
&, walking up the steps, i have nothing to say.

if i tell you quickly: & told quickly,
it will be a truest instance. other times
other such retellings are tautologies,
self-mimes of that better.
i do not admire the plant on the sill, shrivelling.
i do not thank you for dinner: it is the best.

i talk to you as you talk to me.
tomorrow morning now it is,
i leave & walk out of whatever station.

i walk further because it is not whatever time
& the cleaner might not have done the room.
i look at the shops & they are all the same.
i look at people & they all do not look like you.
i'm back; the cheeriest is the pot of daisies
bought whatever days back. i sit on whatever bed.
the room is all disappearing.
i walk out & look at more shops. they are all
very interesting; i don't know what of.
& you are at the door. walking up the stairs,
do you have anything to say to me?

in the quiet of the night

in the quiet of the night
when alert ears pulse sound
i can hear again the words,
the poet i was earlier reading:
he is one person i understand fully.
i understand he is a poet
& i understand his poetry.
i even understand my own knowledge
of this privacy which is public literary study.

the words will move on more swiftly
than tomorrow will be now. & i will
know, in reading again,
i do not know him
or any other, or myself, or that any poetry
is the public transaction that it must be.
& it must be private ultimately.

when last seen

three things he said & her reply
rang with domestic despair.
there he lurked, practising his cruelty.
too suddenly her sadness overwhelmed
&, behind familiar things, a new keen
hate & that, subsiding, erased
her sadness. her regret & shame
seemed to flow through her fingers;
the prepared vegetables definitely tasted
too oily; her snakes-&-ladders emotions
the chequered dishcloth. three times the drain gurgled
& her request rang with clarity.
there he lurked, practising his plumbing.
the snakes & ladders slithered down,
carrot ends & chillie seeds & onion roots.
as he got up she threw the dishcloth,
his face the draughtsboard. she saw distinctly
a softening of his features &, stepping forward,
shed all her tears into the sink.

flying

i had thought the little boy's legs stilts,
arrowing downwards in swift papery rustle.
the stilts moved & upwards the paper soared,
dipped & seemed puckered before a higher lift.
the boy's heart, flying,
its artery the string.

i had thought the stilts little boys' legs
balancing in a pageant. the *papier-mache* head
swollen with a huge grin, following a lion
in the dance. joss-smoke swirling to height,
clowning, balancing, flying.

two women fighting

the thud of a fist preceded the other
woman's scream. then both clung together
& any tiny respite was hair-pulled.
not for a moment could i have thought
they were sisters or friends
hugging away the lapse of a long absence.

two boys fighting proves a point
about football, loving a fight.
& two men fighting in drunken jollity
leaves only a margin of idiocy.
unlike two men fighting
two women fighting leaves no uncertainty.

dinosaurs

After visiting the 1964 New Generations show of paintings and
sculptures at Whitechapel, Keith Vaughan wrote:

> After all one's thought and search and effort to
> make some sort of image which would embody the
> life of our time, it turns out that all that was really
> significant were toffee wrappers, licquorice allsorts
> and ton-up bikes...
> I understand how the stranded dinosaurs felt when
> the hard terrain, which for centuries had demanded
> from them greater weight and effort, suddenly
> started to get swampy beneath their feet. Over-
> armoured and slow-witted, they could only subside
> In frightened bewilderment.

> — Keith Vaughan, *Journal & Drawing*, 1966

the dinosaurs were reactionary;
had no other bulk acceptance
to push back the pace. often inconvenient
& mismanaged, still the world
to them was accustomed kindness;
they basked in the sun which was round & real,
not a suspended soft sculpture, a cybernetic disc.
when the sun changed conceptually
& one more light was piled upon the vatic mind,
they lumbered as they walked, sidled sideways
from toffee wrappers & licquorice allsorts.
the oblique approach was the safest; the truth a gait.
within the cage of modernities, the dinosaurs prowled,
looked for exits: expressed themselves somehow,
sometimes eloquently, crossing the swampy gap
without the help of souped-up bikes.
but no dinosaur could entirely submerge
without resurfacing in a museum,
a new-generation contemporaneity,
as no meaning could go away
without returning upon itself.

street scene i

shaking the match long after it was dead,
as if it were a pioneering gesture for fire,
the man asked of me:
do you know the hours for reduced rates?
i had no such vital knowledge, being a visitor.
putting the match back into the box,
as if it were to be a sealed ecological artefact:
you don't know then, he said with certainty
of my ignorance. i knew i had to check & know
this bit of information, suddenly very necessary.

i did not. but, before i didn't, i watched him,
wearing his woe with a proprietorial air,
walk to someone else. perhaps he asked it again.

of such questioners there are two:
one who goes truly hoping to find answers
& one who secretly hopes he won't.
i think he didn't want to ask anything
except: why am i so lonely & have to stop you?
i felt the same then. as he walked on,
he seemed to grow larger & larger,
ignoring the laws of perspective.

street scene ii

there can never be too many people in the street.
immediate evening, the afterimage is a bitter glow
of neon moons creating their own sky.

the street is neither too long nor too short
for the night, too, is neither.

& by losing oneself, the solipsist's nightmare
in which everything exists but oneself:
a big foveal eye.

foursome

as we were talking, she thrust her head,
regular as a metronome, & rapped orders at him
& the dog. a finger-shaking woman, full of injunction
for man & beast. whenever she called out in her pained
pinched voice, i would watch her, he me, & the dog him.

with the first peal of thunder, the dog raced a circle.
her finger shaking became critical. he turned to lower
a bamboo blind; was shut off. i could see the dog
full of indignation against the thunder & lightning
she was the goddess of. & he, long ago, must have stolen
the first embers to flame his household with little crises,
necessary to outlast all the next days.

exchanges

because he was so old & inexpensively untidy,
the alliteration of the cash register & the fingerer's
ice-cube laughter. she thought the cans of dogfood
were for himself, a damn silly old sod.

she was so painted & bouffant, & her escutcheon
of a skirt wouldn't have hidden a can of worms;
he thought her a whore. up there, dogs, catfood.

through all the month of days, the silent exchanges
raced with the clarity of cellophane over fresh-cut ham.
when he bought watercress, he was a drowning man,
an old dog with a granite collar, a seaweed stew.
her heavy breasts over the keys; no wonder cows play
the yamaha with their udders. what's this chalky liquid
in the plastic bottle? have you given it your all?

to celebrate the cerebral prior to physical potentials:
here's a pot of green syphilitic-looking ceterah,
cakes like trod-on dung, pneumatic mangoes, choices
galore.

alternation

Then, at college, in a single day I decided to change my handwriting... which meant, I realized later, a change in the making of words which even then were all of me I cared to have admired... I sat down with the greatest deliberation and thought how I would make each letter of the alphabet from that moment on...

Well, that change of script was a response to my family situation and in particular to my parents. I fled an emotional problem and hid myself behind a wall of arbitrary formality.

— William Gass, *Writers at Work,*
The Paris Review Interviews

a simple act orthographed with complexity
deliberating shaped lines on paper.
what is it for but oneself, out of joint?

look at the columns of linears deployed
on the surface: should they make cosmetic sense,
no ontogenic sense is gained. the paper cuts something
between them and their beginnings. more powerful,
more sustaining than real-life familiarities;
to appear on one's own screen would vindicate

a whole existence.
                    they exist for the nonce,
these emergent alpha-beta angels & float
in any meaning willed to them. pulsed to a tether,
will you let them

be? or you free?

immediate capsule history; a recognition moves
in memory. they have all been here before.
the brilliant hand radiating a crisp clutch of letters,
too, never forgets where it's been & it's been
over these stretches many many times.
today, there can be ten reasons for the changes,
tomorrow might see another ten new ones.
there isn't a single, disappointing, unchanging answer.

eyes

*I know thy works, that thou art neither cold nor hot: i would thou
wert cold or hot.*

— Revelation 3: 15

i spoke the only words for the entire duration:
thank you, eyes. something troubled,
the eyes were very sad.

either hot or cold, the eyes were very sad.
a rule of eyes: be careful in the search
of adventure, it's very easy to find.

the eyes were sitting there, tidy mental bundles.
the clever eyes, which steal people for their existence,
line a face never creased. never very tidy.

never hot or cold.

nightjar

here, in the night, trees sink deeply downward.
the sound of moonlight walking on black grass
magnifies the clear hard calls of a nightjar,
its soliloquy of ordered savagery, little intervals.
time, clinging on the wrist, ticks it by
but eyes, glued to the dark pages of night,
could not scan the source on the branch.

its insistent calls jab & jab so many times
to a silent ictus, so many times, ringing off the branch
in tiny sharp *tuks*, each lifting from the last

through the night. while the shadows of the trees
go past the edge of sleep & i sit awake,
if it's footfalls across the road, they should be
far away, sounding on the trees, an euphony
lodged on high, the starlit side of heaven.

paraphrase

when one wonders how to begin to talk
about something, the word swallows the world.
the word comes close to carrying its own ontology,
its own reward for being:
        all the way to hakōne
words were hung on every tree. the most striking,
startlingly orange, tuned by the breeze.
words, maple leaves. words were brown moss,
mellow sunlight with soft hair.

words were on the lake; sea-mews spanning circles,
white on white foam of the boat's wake. a translucent
        mist
held the banks in check. then, a sudden reined splash
of muted colour, a shape proffered itself. the image
        beckoned
the eye, a word whispered itself: it's a blue moored boat,
a clump of willows. words were a crocodile of schoolboys
jostling & laughing on the deck.

the lake was a sheet of glass; everything a smaller mirror
beneath. on the surface, a catamaran floated us,
words, all the way to hakōne, words were.

a good poem

*They know how to enjoy themselves without ceasing to be good
boys and girls.*

— Miyuki Nagaoka

so do we.
too, we are good. you, good boys & girls,
how in enjoying yourselves are you
in such completion, mutual absorption.

& how the marvellous colours flow:
your clothes, her scarf, his redolent words.
you are the regenerative peacocks of this world.
today, i am a sparrow pecking at the earth,
the rainbow, the cloud storing a complete typhoon.

excuse us, we also want to go up.
from the huge glass window, the rail tracks
spread out like the ribs of a fan. no,
i don't want a coffee. you are taking me
to mimiu for *udon suki*. let's go down.
the lift is full of good boys & girls.

too.

the shisen-do
A ZEN GARDEN IN KYOTO

you can almost hear the sap raise newer leaves.
past the simple rustic outside-gate,
a slightly ascending passage with stepping-stones
leads to the inside-, the garden front.
the interior garden reveals shaped azalea bushes,
sand combed into a pattern, a spent wisteria,
little white daisies. a low waterfall,
the clacking of the *sōzu*. not too many flowers,
not too many lives.

the woman bending over some plants
thought they were a kind of chrysanthemum,
her words never once staying her tending hands.

no photographer to record the scene, to fail.

a bowl of green tea, a biscuit on a paper square.

always the same tableau, intrinsically still,
the kindling of every sentience.
it is always the same & one can see
it had always been, will be.

12-times table

a scenic depiction is always inexorable
being exclusive right down to its very agencies:
grass, water, sky, hills. the two worlds,
that depicting & that transmogrifying beyond,
beyond grass, water, sky, hills; the two worlds
can come to no direct contact. yet without such contact
no evocation of a transfer is possible:

> an arm for a branch,
> a ear for a sliver of bank,
> an eye for a pod,
> a heart for age-rings.

it was at gifu. it was at osaka.
it was blue-&-white ceramics at gifu;
it was amethyst ceramics at osaka.
camellias, egg-plants, pines: designs of the fingers.
gourds, other forms: shapes of the fingers.
it was here. it was also here

what took place was very possible
without restive rankle of grass, water, sky, hills.

at nagoya
for Kyoko

there is a zoo & botanic gardens combined.
the vernal equinox comes on grey & subdued,
a curiously fluid morning, spring not fully arrived
& things go on their own ways. in the hothouses,
unforced, the theme is verdant crisis.

suave wind, tepid sun outside. bottled,
the heavy-lidded fuschias could explode,
extemporize the greeness of the year & bring with it
a pain, out in the open, need not be endured.

a high pile of glass with its own weather.
a thick pile of clothes with its own arms.
huge cactuses, boys' prickly heads potted.
the steely air lades moisture to the eyes.

where, at nagoya, a zoo & botanic gardens combine,
a portion of time lies waiting.

i can't remember where

i can't remember where, in some part of tokyo,
ripples of water were ringing outwards
in clear cool shivers. again the pond stilled.

a vagrant lying thickly wrapped on a bench;
splinters of sunlight, filtering through a paulownia,
soft-etched his stubbled face orange.

the cackle of wild ducks, fleeing or fled.
a nearby shrine, a tree's slender branches
tied all over with paper charms. a few people
in unhurry. a little rusty bell among grass
didn't tinkle, twice i shook it & threw it
into the pond; hardly a ripple. i peered into it,
my face somewhat startled. a nervous laugh,
as if not from me.

when memory is too much, one turns to the eye;
so i watch the particularities.
in a few days, i shall be going to osaka.
here, a deep contentment is, at once
i want to leave & never look back.
i know it all now; it was closer then.

a peony display, ueno park

how quaint, this woman standing elegantly
& this lush flower a foot below her face.
she turned, the flower bowed.
she sat on a stool, the flower sat
for her brush & reappeared
a soggy sea-anemone.
i suddenly laughed, regretted; the look
of her annoyance, the flower's arrogance.

the afternoon grown heavy,
amidst so many milling people
everything so still, hushed, revered.
yet the peonies maddened the ground
& providence had excluded all other flowers
for them to culminate in grace
& reappear in everybody's face.
they, peonies walked all about.
i sat & watched & watched;
it was time to go.

i walked into a fair at the first corner turned;
it was noise, silent spaces, both linked
by running children. a heavy peony-roiled sky
brimmed over with petals of rain.
everything was a quiet refrain
invisibly tethered to one will.

i am not sure

i am not sure; having walked a half hour
probably in a circle, i'm back here
near the coffee bar. the owner had once given me
a red tobacco cigarette. it was on a poster
&, not knowing japanese, had looked at it
long & hard & hearing some explanation
i couldn't understand, it was given me.
i had puffed it at toranomon station.

here is toranomon, & where shall i go?
the long lines of stalls at ueno? seafood,
pickles, fruit, vegetables. i think of the words
orenzi & *ringo*; not of the paradoxes of oranges
& apples. didn't think it clever. hachiko,
the statue of a dog, at shibuya station?

at the ginza; a side street, the aroma of corn-cobs
blew enticingly from an open wooden cart.
a florist's, bunches of baby's-breath like froth.
displays of food in glass cases; a replica salad
on which perched an iparella leaf.

tokyo is much much for me. i want to leave.
i want to leave without having left
& walk every side street & hear the slurps
the stand-up noodle shops emit.
at the hotel, i dreamt i was in tokyo
&, waking up, was, knew it was time to go
before the tentative become conditional.
& my sleep was without shadows.

a list of things
A MARKET AT UENO

gesticulating fingers of lentil, unwriggly eels,
spearheads of bamboo shoot, soothing water chestnuts,
green snakes of cucumber, jetsams of seaweed,
wrinkled-nose pickles, earspans of brown mushroom,
calm persimmons, outlandish roly-poly apples,
air-licking clams, dry earth-crusts of fish,
icy-eyed bream, powdered kabuki faces of cake,
paragraphs of beancurd, exhaling piles of garlic,
enpurpled piccolo noses of aubergine, lazy grapes,
no-nonsense tangerines, arms-folded-over squid,
shrine-pillars of celery, bullets of green chillie,
hibernating squares of handkerchief, fat tabi,
expandable sweaters, ventilated t-shirts, healthy cod,
alliterative clogs, knobbly topshell, discusses of sole,
lumpy puffy octopus, cheap skate, tight-jaw oysters,
brisk aprons, tough-guy pork, sectional ropes of radish,
whispery crinkled lettuce, placid sweet potatoes,
smarting capsicum, defiant crabs, sensuous musk melons,
humpy peanuts, leathery heels of abalone,
aerial spring onion, hour-glass pears, rotund avocados,
rib-caged pumpkins, chlorophyllic piles of iparella,
grumpy red mullet, macho beef, sassy tomatoes

are all there.

paired stills

at heian shrine
a handpainted kimono
rustled like wild grass

grass sprang from the hem
stopping short of the obi
& walked up those steps

gulls mewing loudly
carry the sunset
from here onto there

there, as seen from here,
banks of white chrysanthemums
spread a slow dawn

those single-peonies
within the reach of our fingers
tantalize the eye

those double-peonies
aching under their own weight
eye us wearily

the slope to the house
is paved with good intentions
to be kind to our feet

so walk up the slope
the house rises on its feet
welcomes us kindly

woman at the bench
two big parcels by her side
her two big achievements

two men at her side
her temporary parcels
their big achievement

so still, butterfly
you are regenerative
a perched amethyst

your eggs on the leaf
soon will spin cocoons & breeze
& so many loves

the riverside inn
serves many little dishes
remarkable us

a brown-green teacup
big as a rather small head
i hold it to mine

right in the centre
red roses named *samurai*
the rest were *rōnin*

even though it's may
a pink camellia
makes its own statement

raked patterns on sand
a little flaw at the swirls
gave it more merit

a white paper cup
thrown among michaelmas daisies
multiplied quickly

at this potter's house
we were offered fried bracken
gathered from the hills

i bought a bottle
picked bracken & mushroom
it contained my hill

the loud clamseller
praises the size of his clams
which grin openly

those baleful fisheyes
but much later it was i
who dreamt of the sea

persimmon trees

bleak november knit its grey bale of sky.
suddenly, a persimmon tree, gnarled, leafless,
hung with acrid orange orbs, flashed by.
the view was from a bus.

later, among the dozens of tomb mounds
of silla kings & queens at kyongju,
more trees, laden with more persimmons;
bigger, more expansive trees.
a shoulder-hoist prankster broke a branch,
arched by the weight of a dozen fruit.
the flurry of a guard,
shouts & protest. ah, tourist, tourist.

in all , an irritation. on the bus,
again more & more persimmon-laden trees,
each a greater dazzle.

i couldn't relate.
the first was persimmon enough.

waterbabies

And what did the little girl teach Tom? She taught
him, first, what you have been taught ever since
you said your first prayers at your mother's knees;
but she taught him more simply. For the lessons in
that world, my child, have no such hard words in
them as the lessons in this, and therefore the
waterbabies like them better than you like your
lessons, and long to learn them more and more;
and grown men cannot puzzle nor quarrel over
their meaning, as they do here on land; for those
lessons rise clear and pure... out of the everlasting
ground of all life and truth.

— Charles Kingsley, *The Water Babies*

other parts of the city, too, are capable of evoking the
          past
lor anyone wishing to walk his imagination a little.
these *klongs* suggest the riverine quantity of life:
wooden huts opening on the water like brown teeth,
theatre sets of a different itinerant age.
buoyant clumps of water hyacinth, tenacious,
hard to separate limb from limb. spawns of water baby
-snails, flotsam, jetsam, cartons printed with bold figures
& colours, variously sinking annealing french letters.

the waterbabies, not to mince meat, are buoyant baby
          tenderloins.
each ensconced in a little boat with a canopy, curtains
& a smile, all drawn discreetly for any descending tom.
a tom descends a bridge. a boat is a vehicle for a tom.
a tenderloin is on the mat. a boy stands at the back,
wielding a long oar, the range of dark water. at the front,
an oil lamp bobs, lit for interaction. & to all this,
a little bridge is a major requirement.

one night, & we walk the night in the bridging
        imagination
of our mind. we imagine that interaction must have been
very inactive. eve or six boats left their bridge,
left the bridging imagination of our mind, & drifted
aimlessly, lanterns bright. all at once, in the darkness,
a waterbaby started crying a plaintive song whose heart
-torn appeal was clear as a bell. another took up the song,
another, the others. in a moment, a full able-bodied
        choir,
a sweet clear siren that reached out nowhere &
        everywhere
& destroyed no one. they were not destroyed that one
        night.
slowly, the bell rippled into the inner vortex of the water.
somewhere, it is still alongside every pecky minor bridge.

denpasar

not surprisingly the bus was brand new.
at the lean-to junction, an assortment of visitors
boarded & then waited. i had expected more from kuta,
one said to her friend. excuse me, the interrupter
had expected less. what do you think denpasar will be
like?
we were going there, our next evaluation.

a boy pedlar, hands & shoulders laden,
his face framing every low window.
cheap, can give discount. what's that? someone pointed
&, turning round, added: i don't go for all that
souvenir crap. what do you want it for? me, i go
for the real yield of the country.
a jam jar, that what's-that, round the boy's waist,
two grasshoppers caught in between waylaying buses.
not for sell.

but that's just what i want.
ok, how much? the boy was adept at extracting rupiahs,
lots & lots of which signified nearly nothing.

denpasar. out onto a square, a perfect square
of brown earth; grass was thoroughly absent.
ah, the grasshopper asked, perhaps seeing
in it whatever he wanted: & you know what?
we knew as, at once, he ripped off the string-tied leaf
& the grasshoppers sprang away after several feeble leaps.
what you do that for? not surprisingly:
to give them their freedom. what else you think?
i thought i saw people & insects hobble-hop, hobble-hop
over the burning earth. their freedom, it was true,
was right under the generosity of the hot hot sun
right over the world at bali.

cianjur

the woman & buffalo at a distance were so still.
rice seedlings would have grown from her fingers
if she had not hurried on. an extravagant sunset.
lush flowers, the decaying smell of the wooden house;
rotting balcony, moss-legged cane furniture.
the serial chirping of insects. a naked bulb,
later lit; the pool of ants' wings a prayer mat,
this day's announcement of approaching darkness
thick & crepy as a physicality.

the inside of the house was its outside in reverse.
clumsier rotting furniture. nothing worked, dry taps,
the telephone in a smoulder of dust.
an empty, empty hoariness; & its own despair.

all around the house, tall trees, vine-clung,
wild jasmine located by scent, chequer-board
padi fields. slope upon slope,
undulating till the last touched a level
& took away with its splendour one's breath;
a sere coconut leaf javelined the ground.
runner plants fingered their way &,
touching the house variously, never let go.

the distant orange sun taught different greens
for different identities. acid-green seedlings,
sunsteeped tree greens, brown greens, orange greens,
the violent green of a streaking kingfisher.
green noises from wet fields;
the eeriness floating off the hills, green ghosts.

& green were we when we got here
miles from anywhere, this dilapidation
described to us as a chalet-style hotel;
this ruin being hugged by all this grandeur
& gradually being strangled for not being a part.
mutually encroaching, it could not vanquish.
it could be vanquished.
it could be very vanquished
before our eyes.

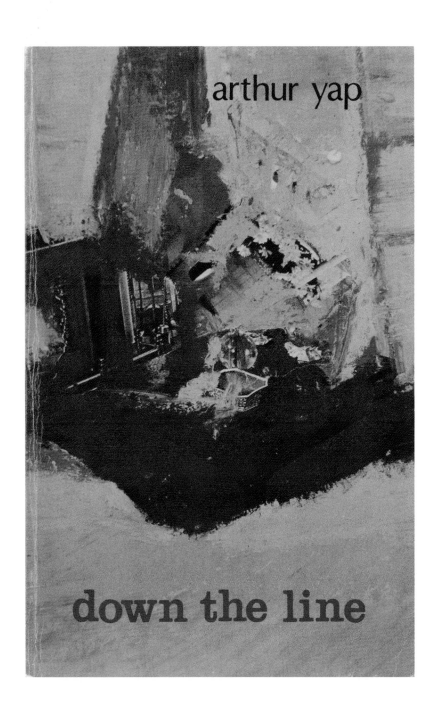

arthur yap

down the line

DOWN THE LINE
1980

they are days

days are variable,
each day has what each day has.
that, which others haven't,
is best. its best is more
a constant. less best
is less everything lenitive.

they are variable,
each they has what each they hasn't.
this, which others have,
is better. but best is more
a concern. less best
is plus everything fugitive.

paper

paper explains many things.
its surface is skin
above-bone, grafted at eye-level.

egyptian papyrus,
chinese rice paper,
epidermis, stationers',
bonds, suicide notes,
minutes of meetings.
the latter 2 may be (maybe) writ in blood.

plastics takes many years to decompose.
paper doesn't, all the time endless succession:
heroes & villains who've rocked the boat
wade (only) downwards to find it,
not mud, is paper-given.
& freedom is paper. upwards, too,
every cloud has a papery lining.

shipwreck

shipwreck: i've written about it, & more, before.
with an island background, it had only been composed
upon in school. splendid shipwrecks, salted treasure
as easily scooped, a misgrounded fly from an ink-bottle.
the scope of fluent ignorance, my pen raced. at that age
i chased themes that were totally mine, weren't dreams.
it was a duty owed more myself than the pen.

about shipwrecks: were i in school now, i'm better able
to write on the velocity of wind, oscillations of tides,
the extent of salvage insurance companies need underwrite,
the structural implications on shocked timber.
can't i?

nowadays teems with more themes.

sheepwreck: (as i imagine) in animate collision,
each impact cushioned. do i say to you:
let us not pull wool over each other's eyes
(& other civilities)?
over to the ships' wrecked captains where it seemed
to have begun & then definitely ended,
to pirates marinated in seasonal winds,
to a harbour where eyes obtain like sardines:
a shipwreck is a tall shore of humanity.
with an island background, it had been composed
on sand, dry inland, crafted by hand.
it can be seen in the city, daily,
neatly.

medium

behind the fence-struggling morning-glory, you see 2 trees:
one is a fig tree, the other a (smaller) fig tree.
below one or the other sits a kampung chicken
equipped with a telephone, with or without an extension,
the kampung chicken's mouth is its lower effusion,
each time it squiggles, some shit (surely) drops out.
below the tree, this one or that, the telephone rings,
the kampung chicken squeals with delight over the
information.
listen, listen to how the leaves zing with activity.

the kampung chicken is itself a clearing house,
yesterday's lain egg is dead. it exults over such hatch
because, from that, it knows it existed yesterday,
that yesterday hadn't been a sloppy omelette.

behind the fence-hugging morning-glory, you see 2 trees:
one is a grapevine, the other a (quicker) grapevine.
look at the kampung chicken, it pimps for every ring
& prinks properly over every prime prize ping.

statement

of course your work comes first.
after that, you may go for a walk,
visit friends but, all the same,
it is always correct to ask
before you do anything else.

so if you say: please may i jump
off the ledge? & go on to add
this work is really killing,
you will be told: start jumping.
no one is in any way
narrow-minded anymore these days.
It is that everyone likes to know
these things way beforehand.
but if you state: i'm going now,
jumping off the ledge
most probably they will say nothing
thinking should it legally, morally,
departmentally, be yes/no/perhaps.
or if it's not too late:
why don't you come along? we shall bring
this matter up to a higher level.

dramatis personae

i. public park

along the bench we're variations of a line
that watch the many flowers grow
into our understanding, & die
because we're not to pick them.
they are for the public.
we in public are private figures
humanizing the landscape
on the little hill. under the trees
we listen for the millennium
while following the turn of the floral clock
with the knock of a new plastic heart.
this park is self-centred
it takes & it rejects.

this park is self-centred
& outsiders just get in the way.
today you are in the park
waiting for us, watching us
young men & women, old boys & girls,
parking ourselves. (how we laugh).
how we laugh & then cry,
since we bring you some happiness
you should also have some of our sadness.

ii. public beach

where does the road end & the beach begin?
It is not easy to say, so closely
do the 2 forms intermingle.
blending the neat sharp smell of petrol
with the warm scent of dirty sand.

here is the sand,
& further from the sand
(can you see?)
here is the sea.
sand & sea are less today
as there is more of life.

webbed up here by the sewer
sewn to the hardness of cement
trapped by piss-moss, little landcrabs
are more crust than crab & salt.
& caught here, we would never have been
more than all these things we have seen.
that cemented here, as we are not,
we run away before the waves arrive
with a little last fresh collapse.

iii. public pond

coming down to the very bank
the soil is very old & crumbly.
you would not laugh
seeing it so, for it is yours.
today you are a pond, a still pond
hoping for the little boys to happen
there with their jars, here with their nets.
they drown
because you are too abstract
when they bend over you
searching among weeds for what they want
before they turn to conceits, the lesson
on fish & waterlife & diagrams,
with no waterdrops of agitation on their hands.

it is important they come each sunday
replacing the week's gloom with their faces.
in you they drown, an old familarity,
& they will rise again day after day
after this, like some terrible fish.
their simplicity is your certainty.

down the line

i.

the wind that weaves across buildings
carries the calculus the city is reckoned on.
call it what we will, it is liquid graphics,
neither statistics nor logistics can propel,
for its basis well under the skin has yet another
lined in rubrics & this, then, is palpable
& lends the eye whatever enchantment it wishes.
it will enchant with the cool young shadows
the sun, climbing vertically down windows,
leaves behind. it will enchant in its repose
by moving, shifting to the centre of its axiom,
in its layering of reality & in imparting
the sum of its being; every part, every space
larger & more real than the entirety.
if tomorrow someone sings a confessional
of some 'ism or other, the refrain sinks in
as only a totality & any event, being given,
predetermined, is at the onset already silent.
silently, the moon flanked by ribbed clouds
is jailed for influencing, or not, missiles
& this too holds no stored fear for tomorrow
it rains & the gurgling of drains, protomusic,
will soothe ancient nerves, iron out new alarms.

ii.

we say that a person who had stabbed himself
19 times & then thrown his own body over
the balcony is unbelievable reportage.
if you tell me times enough, tired, i will believe
or, at the least, agree. & if you tell me
times more, angered, i will throw
the narrated body back at you.

possible, too, i well might have believed.
so credulity is a bigger commodity than credibility
which is everybody's. the other, an exercise
of the mind, is yours if you can shape it.
breaking it, breakage is accidental
& never really necessary. a place-style
of impelling rhetorics, down the line,
foisting tautologies as ramifying definitions.

iii.

the tanned figures on the beach are not there
for further sun. noon, the heart's pulsation
without speech, is already late enough.
tenacious as weed, the crabs secrete bricks
& lay at the water's edge a library of margins.
page by page, it prefabricates the day's
ins & outs but, like pure callisthenics,
seem never quite enough. created thus to grow,
the calculus will help or quell us.
i thought the ground had foretold all.

a habit by which the world moves, people will not
look at the centre of things. the custodian must
find some flaw about his own belief to show up
those, accusing him, as punitive. wrong,
that in his pursuit, he does them good
purely by chance. such coincidence is a gift
&, in these days of libs, isn't it lib & let lib?
when the verb fails, everything ancillary
has only its chronicle of current antiquity.

grass replaces grass, fast. down the line,
dry, roots are cast. garden-to-garden green grass
calls to the eye an explication of beauty
& beauty, in the colouring heart of the beholder,
is not what suffices or does not. that it does not
comes last.

iv.

what everyone will tell you is what everyone
wants to hear, has been told. the clouds
have no radio & cannot relay silver linings,
glosses, appendices. we hear, what told,
wheels of woe, a battery of ear-assault
pooling in the lymph. the years,
if they have brought us no wisdom, would have
exploded the myth our images hold, rearranged
the calefaction of the thermometer
we regulate by.

the dove

he can fly across all oceans & skies
be attacked by automatons
public relations
& still be in one peace.

night scene i

the warmth had left the west. timid
the stars appeared. preparedly, in the distance
a finger of light waved across the sky.
others too appeared &, higher or lower,
all impressed their lines on the blackboard sky.
quickly they are disambiguated,
the solitary finger is left
to write the margin of the next sunrise.

night scene ii

the roofs drank in all the stars.
from the high evacuated space of sky,
visual acuity: tiny ambient arrows,
eyes opening like daisies
tomorrow. on the promenade,
soggy stars. one day later
the place is young again,
stars hooking up the roofs
in the high evacuated space of sky.

would it have been

would it have been different if it were not an apple
but a bomb which bit the world into being

&, whatever the conditionals, would it be different
after the bite, the lingua franca of the world
were sign language, metalanguage, antilanguage,
argot, braille, ipso facto esperanto,

houses were nests & people prefabricated
soyabean sculptures,

sunlight falling on a field burnt grass
into terminal rainbows,

cities held to ransom by their own devils
or collective dream sequences

: would it be very different if all these things
have had being been untrue?

a lesson on the definite article

a crowded restaurant, open eavesdropping
graded into one another's ears. sharing table:
a bearded man, a girl with bank-teller's eyes;
they arrived after me, & an umbrella & 2 coats
which were there when i was.

i really love chinese food, you people can cook
beautifully. the bearded man had also a large appetite.
i can't cook, & her non-sequitur
'the poor chinese are like the 2nd class jews'
provoked these possibilities:
poor chinese are like 2nd class jews,
poor chinese are like the 2nd class jews,
the poor chinese are like 2nd class jews.

the she was, by the way, the chinese
& her the accent, showing she had arrived,
gone the places, reached the it,
made the it, confirmed she was the.

the grammar of a dinner

let's have chicken for dinner.

somewhere else, someone else utters:
let's have john for dinner.
we are alarmed by the latter
but a dinner, too, has its own grammar
& we are assured by grammarians
both utterances are in order.

john, + animate, + human,
couldn't be passed off as repast.
chicken is + animate, – human,
& can end up in any oven.
if we combine the items of grammar
the way things in cooking are,
we would then have:
let's have chicken for john for dinner,
let's have chicken for dinner for john,
let's have for john chicken for dinner,
let's have for dinner for john chicken;
but probably not:
let's have john for chicken for dinner,
let's have for dinner john for chicken.

john is a noun holding knife & fork.
chicken collocates with the verb eat.
grammarians favour such words
as delicious & john eats happily,
but in a gastronomic dinner
taxonomic john isn't to eat deliciously.

event

a little combed & frilled girl, smile older,
at her wedding, the aunt's. combed & frail,
smile smaller, the bride's teeth stuck to her gums.
the occasion gave it beauty.

combed & frilled, the bouquet (waved about
like a microphone) picked up congratulations.
hands down, on the table 2 gloved mice.
(& another piece of peking duck for you?)

event.
eventually, the bride will be
at the little girl's wedding.
& peking ducks will get eaten
by other 2 gloved mice
in careful pieces.

roll call

i can understand animals in a zoo:
aren't they for our enjoyment?
i can understand their entertainment:
if they turn a few tricks for us
do we not give them some peanuts?
i cannot understand the zoo in me:
why i eat peanuts, am sometimes absurd.
i understand why i cannot be a zoo:
first of all, i wear glasses.
next, i don't particularly like mud,
turd & other such esoterica.
&, finally, i'm not very sure
of the heuristics of such phrases:
'social interaction' & 'behavioural objectives',
which i hear often
& which seem applicable to all animals.
because i can't understand them
i want to object to the phases
of (be)having to interact with them.
believing they must do their thing(s),
there'll always be a zoo. i shall go on
giving them peanuts & eat some myself
(not necessarily simultaneously)
)& would you like some as well?(

samson & delilah

they gave her a pair of scissors to cut his hair.
she didn't & they made love, there on the floor.
the bedridden grandmother wondered why the young,
always so noisy, were then fighting on the floor.
she must ask that boy never to come again.

the parents, on the rise, are breeders of girl guides,
they grow more grave as they grow more serious.
the youngsters, she is theirs, rising, are gone.
but she, who is theirs, will ask him to come again, soon.

worse & worse,
his hair not shorn. the other parents were afraid
their district was being given a bad image.
bad image: that noisy boy, on the floor,
hair shorn, listening to the rolling stones.
they didn't need give her scissors anymore.
she hadn't, & they made love, there on the floor.
the bedridden grandmother was dead,
dead to the noisy fight. hair shorn, gone
was the need to keep the long-standing irritation
over all other ordinary human volition.

parts of speech

coming upstairs with a bag of toilet rolls
he was ashamed to see me. i'm just the cleaner,
i clean your room & all the others in this wing.
i can get a job anywhere else, you know,
it's just that i happen to like it here.

last semester a student,
he didn't need clean his own room.
it's just that i'm not good in my work
& messed up every damn thing.

in the dining hall, busy with pleasantries,
everyone a student or studying something,
working for a degree or some other weighting.
ted, residential cleaner, had a bag of such paper.
at 3 successive dinners i heard him say
i'm just the cleaner, you know. then,
want to go to the union for a drink?
when i said yes, he said let's make it
tomorrow when he said let's call it off.
later, he rationalized over the cancellation
of his own invitation: it can't be
because of my head that he wants
to be friends with me, you know.
it can't be because of my clean status
(you know he can be, additionally, witty).
& he reasoned that i must be
after some of his other parts.

a family movie

theda is an anagram for death
& bara a near-palindrom for arab.
she, lapping up this bit of movie news,
wants to call herself thus.
we shall call her eve.

i much prefer it in front,
it's rather like death behind, she said
to adam about seats in the cinema.
another day, she groped for adam's cork
screw, dropped among thick picnicking grass.
adam bit greedily into her nut
cake, his appetite unrepentant.
o don't stop don't stop, eve said,
i don't want remnants tomorrow.
it's the best tit
bit i've had, bara none, adam said.

baldilocks & the 3 heirs

hair today, gone tomorrow:
age's song sung. each day
a pate here
a crown there
absence makes the scalp flounder.
a snip here
a snip there
removal makes the face rounder.
baldilocks with 3 hairs
turned corner
of his 50th year.
ear here
ear there
his smile grows larger
his social mileage more comfortable.
frizzy & frizzled
flakes on the shoulders,
a scowl here
a growl there
the 3 heirs
raze the business
the father had raised.
facing bankruptcy
a lawsuit here
hirsute there
generative of much bad air.
: baldilocks & the 3 heirs
& all the family:
this isn't a story.

window view

the way the dummy
glassy with eyes
stared out of the bowl
filled with acrylic weed
at the window all the time
made me wonder
if someone hadn't let
the goldfish out & instead crafted
an aquarium from this little shop
in the podium block
showing all & sundry
this shopping centre
offers also novelty
in addition to the idiocy
that there are hundreds of shops
in dozens of other centres
offering similar multiplicities
in thousands of windows
for onlookers to gaze at
& then let only their eyes swim in.

topnote

the glint of sun is from bronze-floated windows
skyscraping lesser buildings & some trees awaiting
resiting. very seldom is the building's immensity
more prominent when, at early evening,
the spacing of red chases the bronze to a closed tone,
less metallic glass than a structural cue.
do not add eyes to the windows. a faraway plane,
a greyish isolate, gives better closure. the space
between it & the building linked in apparent time,
a cool medium this superordinate thing.
nevertheless, it requires completion every evening.

old tricks for new houses

can't adjust to the glare of white sand.
these dunes, disappearing when the estate appears,
now run chokey rivulets & a water-margin,
halting at exposed roots, outlines a future fence.
when the gate clangs with the hand, it is now
the presumption of a future tense.
everything tentative in the rain, these tyre marks
will dissolve & leave behind a parquet floor.

the sea can't reach you now
& it'll be further away next year.
your neighbours will hang crabshells
on their pomegranate plants as saline testimony,
your proximate goodwill will be good
& help salt away the years in happy homes.

kilograms

when 2 fat persons get together
the occasion is nearly always one
of creamcakes & verbalism.
the verbalism is on dieting.
creamcakes, an extension of the tongue,
are there because: why not?

when 2 lean persons get together
the occasion is nearly always one
of verbalism & fat persons.
the verbalism is on anything.
the fat persons, expansively lean,
are there because: why not?

the mouth

a one-person theatre of the absurd
is coming my way. i've seen it before
so there's no reason i shouldn't, again. the theme,
like beckett's 'not i', a mouth.
that, alone, is everything.
ears are definitely out;
absurd, the notion that the mouth should want
to listen to any person. its own best marvel,
the mouth takes in everything that moves.
you want to watch it,
you don't want to be on the next intake.
no reports of this marvel
have been disseminated but this isn't the same
as it is in hibernation.

names, dates, faces & (especially)
designations are never forgotten. remembering
with some trepidation the 3rd person, left,
2nd row, disgraced, the mouth will now tell
the image to go away. person: image: face:
these are mere facts & can be questioned,
altered to recognition by new specifications.
the mouth is very alive & very well.

nearly there

in one fallen swoop, hands locked legs.
the ball merrily went onto others'.
legs trod hands, stooped in spread:
one player, out of action, out of field.
swift mobilization, realized in action.
columns, up & down, zig-zagged tracks
hard to match. nearly there.

vanishing the prompts,
left in the dark,
a candle's mental horsepower:
blind sports to fill the hour,
the fluid geometry of power.
each knock enacts the theorem of a pass,
acts on a moment's dare or keeps back
the extended foot, orbicular on the grass.

rsvp regrets only

the ability to read road maps
or do sums, for example, can be described
in terms of an invitation.
one can always ask a further question
about any invitation: what's the good
of learning placenames, peoplenames, & how many
litres are there to the gallon?
unasked, regrets only.

the trouble, though, is that of deciding
what sort of thing is necessary to make
an invitee's autonomy. is it logically
necessary to be unable to prattle,
flip a drink neatly down, or what?
the card in invitational &, therefore, purportedly
carries a value, judgement it does not.
not that it means
regrets are what are being invited.
it is, after all, a filler problem.
the ability to read a number,
use a dialling finger, for example, can be
circumscribed in terms of a contingency.

gallery scenario

upstairs a god (small g, he isn't pleased)
who, sometimes coming downstairs,
finds the offering not laid, his little servants
asleep in their faith.
the alphabetical god comes after cod
(pre-sod) & his array, a range
of baroque psychological nuances
is comely in a consumer society.
the god has, is, does.
others, who haven't, aren't, don't,
don't rate unless they utterly haven't,
aren't, don't, & the god then has largesse.
the god, himself permutated,
owns himself a dog & the alphabetical dog
comes after cog (pre-hog).
the god eats the dog.
eating another isn't wrong
& it's much practised to wit.
the dog eats the god & eating
isn't wrong, is an appetite to boot.
yanked out by its canine roots
& transplanted in the increasingly technical
field of sociability, inevitably a knowhow
develops. & there is greater need
for greater & greater precision
until there is bound to be homage.
whether goddogs are pictured in their ways,
& it is seldom done,
they often outline their own stipulative portraits
& these, too, have a certain format
that very seldom can undergo external ruffling of fur.

open road

breasting a tall crest of road
the sky looms. quick capricious illusion
pushes away 2 banks of rubber trees.
this looming sudden expanse
gathers itself like a sullen face
which over the plantation breaks,
unfurling tight-curled tips of the topmost leaves
with slip-drops of water falling, scattering
lean dogs with humpy shivers.

only the cyclist's heart
halts at the sightless road, wet with eyes.
wet with life, the plantation is its difference
from dry days, defineable days
of heat & light lallang seed.
while the grass usually sizzles with blade-rubs
it now bends green arches under an uncertain rainbow,

the road slices through 2 lives
which are the quick &, mainly, the quicker.

in memory of) anthony

your coffin had no nails.
years i have lived with this nailed feeling,
every moment forgotten. & other moments,
larger remembrances, are also of you.
when all is said & not forgotten,
may it be known to me
& leave behind, not necessarily
even a need to understand
what you all along would know,
this long, long trail of quick, sharp sorrow.

for...

The world is too much with us; late and soon,
                                    — Wordsworth

never late. the current world is too soon.
my parents: one retired, one a housewife,
protected now as they have protected. all along
they have, after all, some of us,
our antiquated smallpoxes. our current problems
they cannot understand & why need they?

right now, i wish for them
what i think i can do, but don't
& they, i don't know if i'm right,
won't accept because they have
given & we, having taken,
now wanting to give, find it all given.
my parents, i'll never give you roses,
jade, accolades (or other such nonsense).
when it clarifies, i'll offer whatever
& i know it will be only a token
of what you, all along, have given.

until

until anthony passed away
i never saw cheeriest optimism
a person leaving hospital,
family carrying bags & he himself.

words

words have sometimes a way of stilling themselves
& then, no, we have a way of stilling words
in a way to still ourselves:
a choice of being still
& quiet to be still.

words need people to fill their blanks,
quick eye-flicks across the page:
a page of contained dimensions
housing a pharynx
that, from edge to edge,
is still,
still as a minute glottal sphinx.

elementary pieces

the simplicity of the elements,
nevertheless, is not to be trusted.

the fluidity of air,
tranquil even as water,
scatters hopes like litter.
simple (as) water,
nevertheless, drowns. & earth,
kind as ever, receives every fall
& glosses over all with a mantle
of grass & flowers.
& any offering, made to fire,
is the day's communion with ashes.

postlude

the morning when requiem for her husband,
newly dead, was said, the evening saw
her new bridal gown brushing up the aisle.

little was said. the few guests at the reception
heard the bride, laughing, would keep her bouquet.
she wouldn't throw it, like defence, at their faces.
her & his children were eating cake.

stepped-down greys

reedy spirals of joss-stick smoke
fingered every background object into grey.
stepping down, the bowing monk is gone,
gone from his lips the articulation of paid lament.
stepped-down greys & the night,
perhaps so dark, no light seemed sharp enough.
twice, like dimmed headlamps, the candles
in the temple yard collided with the soggy moon.
a light breeze floated down & rummaged some leaves
indifferently. last year's calligraphic blessing,
greying on yellow paper, sent reticulations
down the footnote history of the wall.

smaller world

saw,
long after their contention,
disgruntled leaders honing differences
& different followers & parti pris
tenaciously perpetuating their vagaries.

saw them
describing tight big little circles,
each a sufficient world with its own rigour.

saw them
in their worlds. each against each
is but half of one topic
(call the world whatever, some a real need)
in a pre-mortem deadlock.

& seeing
communications make the world small,
saw the smaller world
of sawn partisanship.

nature study

the tree moaned in a series of multiple snaps,
slowly collapsed, & a quick feeble rebound
as if to stand again. its branches are earthed
& the roots branches laden with earth.

a familiar picture. though not seen everyday,
the first once is ancient visualization.
one keeps perhaps an inner reservation:
a private rehearsal of leaves & branches.

take away the seeming branches & the real
you have a trunk that is bidirectional.
growing upwards, falling downwards
(confusion).
you have a trunk that is bilocational,
pointing to lichfield rd & serangoon garden.
you have workers acting as if swearing
were a concrete object they've patented.
the trunk, moved in installments,
may come partly to you.
the frame around the picture
of trees & idyllic nature,
of trees & more trees,
of trees & sky.
there is still a choice.

mime

because the learner sat down
& regurgitated like an open book
para qua para he was taken as a clown.
he wasn't praised for his neat memory.

when the clown stood up
& gurgled like an open sewer
line by line he was taken as funny.
he was praised for his neat mimicry.

because mime is excruciation
ransacking each gesture is eristic.
because excruciation is excruciating
masks that appear in real situations
are worse, & what comparison is possible
when every mask wears a face?
faces mime faces mime faces.

late-night bonus

several teenagers, gathered together
for some organized disorder, have pushed over
a bin & were dancing round our (un)broken bottles.
jostling & shouting, it was quickly over.

of all a sudden i heard midnight laughter,
the 3-houred teenagers back with bicycles.
then jangling bells were quickly gone with the riders.
i remained awake & by linking the sense of speed
with darkness, the sense of place seemed destroyed.
the physical world will return tomorrow
but a moment's loss will not be gone.
& public durances & private aftermaths
every street has known.

a solid laughter theirs, however.

traffic

asked the way to park street
the old man drew himself up,
his shell of woollens seemed unburdened
&, fully intent to edify,
at great pains & greater length ...

like any big city, this city
offers her people a variety of ways
in which moments of unhurry
may be used. the old man knew
roads never look like themselves,
edging sideways from the curb,
pushing over zebra zips. nevertheless ...

& done. rounding a corner a little quicker
than cars, one's eyes read the restaurant's menu
for 'long soup' & 'short soup'.
feet, hesitating speculatively,
are like the feet on the cinema poster,
'porcelain anniversary', a french
concoction of limbs. simulated coitus,
long soup, streaking cars
blue to the gills, brick-clogged pores:
a connection of many things
that cannot undergo any physical editing.

most of october

the landscape is too empty. it threatens to dissolve
& include me in it. it threatens in a series of vast sizes
&, above all, in its indifference. the huge vastness
is always enlarged by some motion: a bird in flight,
a dazzlingly white sail slicing like a slow penknife.

seen through a huddle of wind-torn bushes at cliff edge,
the extravagant surf below pounds a silence to completion.
i cannot hear anymore the amplitude of wing,
wind & other sea-wounds.

the first thing to do is to drop a stone down the cliff
without dropping myself. i don't quite fit into this
landscape & there aren't even trees to give
a similar vertical accent. it needs entire absorption
& i'm not sure i want to throw away my shoes
as a start. i look at the sudden influx of sails
& it's almost like painting by numbers.
but before each square is begun
the others are already marvellously completed.

sights

the sights are like every city's offerings.
the difference is that, here, it is possible
to combine country & sea, a lovely
bilocation for the economy tourist.

on the hydrofoil, you know land
isn't distant. every cliff has a pair of hands:
the stone, the flower, nothing undefined
in the profile. birds cry across the bridge.
the evening sun walks up the cove
& drops smartly into slopping eyes.
you can hear your own fascination.

you turn a corner to a choked car's strangulation
&, from somewhere, a carried peal of bells.
sunsteeped stained-glass, the old enchantment
doesn't hold. at the turnstile, you may remember
something small: a packet of handmade paper
in a shop, a pinecone among grass,
how the coin spun & spun in the booth.

an accumulated store of sights,
the miniscule compress of days, the lovely passage
of quiet water, upward wind.

fog sculpture by fujiko nakaya, the domain

isn't mind-blowing
& nothing actually to see,
at worst may aggravate catarrh.

bright sunny day
with trees, grass & sky
& now a numinous haze
effulgent from concealed hose
rises in the park,
softens outlines of children's gambols,
muffles laughter expectantly surprised.

was it for this we came?
& for this we wouldn't have wanted
ourselves missed. we were the sculpture.

at balmain

quota of dogshit here & there
& the noon absence of dogs.
an old couple sunning
in an ornate wrought-iron porch
(paint peeling like leathery skin)
watched us assemble camera & tripod
with curiosity growing. the old woman,
hard of hearing, rapped out at the man,
her eyes never once moving from us:
what are they doing?
are they television?
& then to us:
gosh, aren't you started?
gosh, now i know who you are,
you can film the whole street for all i care.

i don't remember what the film was about,
every frame, anyway, out of focus. but etched clearly
in memory, the old woman's curlers
danced the way to the wharf
& became giant crests of waves.
the old man's toothlessness
the open space of the nearby park,
& a sibilant breeze
rapidized from balmain's throat.

wayang kulit

cool it baby
this is a cultural show.
before you you see your own shadows:

his introduction was the distilled wisdom
of a hundred conducted tours.
flippancy came easily to disguise
& mock that uncertainty
of audience reaction to a scene
already familiar but unspectacular.
dark cages of shadow
give nothing to go by
but, with such things,
one suddenly knows that, no, not order,
but disorder is drama. & drama
is obligatory human nutrition.

koolit baby
this cultural show is not for you.

a family visit

today's the sunday i visit a typical family
as a typical overseas visitor.

i get the feeling she would rather sit back
& watch tv with curlers in her hair
than prepare a typical meal for me.
& why shouldn't she? the food i'm to eat
she has eaten many times before, & the places
i'm to see he has seen many times before.
like children who, fond of school,
welcome more their vacation,
i am their today's homework.

is there anything about places to visit
or a typical family life i'd like to know?
no, i'm here only for the food.
aloud, i asked about something
& sat 2 hours for the answer with details.

i don't know if i'll like the drive after lunch.
should i come across traffic offences,
would i have to log these as typical?
i don't know if i'm enjoying the drive
& if they are enjoying my ears.
i shall be happy to get back
& have some typical sleep
with or without snores added in the programme.

the centre

buildings, shadows,
locked-in stillness:
sunday & city centre
& one's own subordinate presence.

on sunday it isn't whether the sun
& shadows have been well constructed,
they are a detachable presence.
the other days have the colours of the world.
sunday's recitation is by omission
rather than by commission.
if you had asked, the roadsweeper
would have lent you his road.
it is the day the wheel is re-invented
to a halt.

here then...

here, then. walk in this street,
an area largely migrant.
migrants, definable as migrants
unless integrated: a new norm
is set. no longer confused by audibilities,
old migrants, the new locals, weave
current standards which years ago
they themselves would have found objectionable.
& violations of which they now find unacceptable.

here then is a gradual disposal of folky variables.
the core can always be sold as ice-cones,
hotdogs & other tacky culturals.

i think (a book of changes)

when we came, it was all for grabs;
you might say the motivation was a quick dollar.
then those men came & demanded monthly payments
for 'your protected interest'. it makes life hard,
harder when you think of the pilferers.
a shirt here, a length of material there —
all gone as if into thin air.
but all this has gone on since those television
emperors' tombs & so the protection & the pilferage
isn't the story of this market.
the story is the story of change.

some people give you $5 & ask for change
from 50. this month, french knit is popular.
made in hongkong, the label's changed to u s a.
you don't wrap things up in straits times
or nanyang siang pau anymore, brown paper
isn't even good enough. change to plastic bags,
said one customer, with a pattern of red flowers
for luck. we've changed our name 3 times.
first, 'sincere shirts' was considered common.
everyone's sincere about business, so why be blatant?
next, we called it 'lucky store'. one week later,
my wife found another such store in the next section.
the owner had died. so when we were rightfully
the only lucky, we didn't want to be.
now we call it as it is: 'ah beng fabrics'.
next year we go over to that tall block,
7th floor. we shall call it 'number one stop'.
got to time in with the changes.
what?
what do i think of it?

2 mothers in a h d b playground

ah beng is so smart,
already he can watch tv & know the whole story.
your kim cheong is also quite smart,
what boy is he in the exam?
this playground is not too bad, but i'm always
so worried, car here, car there.

at exam time, it's worse.

because you know why?

kim cheong eats so little.

give him some complan. my ah beng was like that,
now he's different. if you give him anything
he's sure to finish it all up.

sure, sure. cheong's father buys him
vitamins but he keeps it inside his mouth
& later gives it to the cat.
i scold like mad but what for?
if i don't see it, how can i scold?

on saturday, tv showed a new type,
special for children. why don't you call
his father buy some? maybe they are better.

money's no problem. it's not that
we want to save. if we buy it
& he doesn't eat it, throwing money
into the jamban is the same.
ah beng's father spends so much,
takes out the mosaic floor & wants
to make terazzo or what.

we also got new furniture, bought from diethelm.
the sofa is so soft. i dare not sit. they all
sit like don't want to get up. so expensive.
nearly two thousand dollars, sure must be good.

        that you can't say. my toa-soh
        bought an expensive sewing machine,
        after 6 months, it is already spoilt.
        she took it back but.......... beng,
        come here, come, don't play the fool.
        your tuition teacher is coming.
        wah! kim cheong, now you're quite big.

come, cheong, quick go home & bathe.
ah pah wants to take you chya-hong in new motor-car.

a vicious circle

mrs lim (to mrs fernandez):

i don't know what is wrong
but it is all his fault,
through these 30 years, one thing i know:
one should offer only half the cake
& horde up the other bit.
the children are grown & can't be tied,
they are themselves, they have their lives to lead.
my husband — age has made him light
& young at heart. striving to satisfy all his itch,
each morning he returns reeking of that bitch.

    mr lim (to mr song):

    the old woman's grumpy & irritable.
    her overruling passion now is the mahjong table
    where she exercises daily in high fervour
    & the only time she speaks to me is when she wants
    more money, for the household, of course.
    what is life if i have no time to enjoy myself?
    i can't possibly spend my money after i'm gone.

ah lan (to herself):

when it happened last year, i've done
my duty for my mother. she's at least
provided for. he is old & rich,
doesn't make heavy demands on me.
his wife is old & ugly & if i show him
some tenderness, he'll leave me all his money.
then chong, strong & young & fit,
will take me back & make up for the deficit.

mr lim (to himself):

lan is some consolation, she is tender & kind
& therefore a fraud. i believe she despises me
while we are at that. but no matter,
she shall inherit just the siamese cat.

mrs lim (to her husband):

no one knows my sorrow. that young tart
is shrewd & keen, she'll make off with everything.
who cares about me? mrs fernandez
only wants to win at mahjong from me.
let me have some marketing money.

ah lan (to mrs song):

the amah is disgusting & despises me,
i shall sack her when he's dead & gone.
& i shall move house & learn to play the piano.
i won't be great but, at least, i am cultured.
my money will set chong on his feet.
when he's at work, i'll help in the charities,
kissing the sick & being photographed with v i p's.
if i'm helpful & generous, i shall be motioned
to cut the ribbon on special occasions.

fiscal ear

mr song, on the telephone, lets known
he's the head of the organizing committee.
he wonders why the caller wants to be so stingy.
does he not know how to do things in style?
mr song, on the telephone, will have none of that,
nor unnecessary worries: don't worry,
what you want to be so stingy for?
make sure there's plenty of v s o p.
mr song, on the telephone, orders smoked duck,
braised scallop with kai lan & many others
without need to consider any fiscal bother.
who wants to eat sweet & sour pork these days?
you want to eat sweet & sour pork?
& 4 taiwanese singers too, 3 are neither
here nor there.

mr song, later at home, wonders who has given them
those presents strewn on the table: who gave us
all these presents? mr song, at home, shouts
about the purchases his wife got from the emporium:
you think i print money? he wonders if his wife
thinks he prints money & whether she thinks
they're holland rd millionaires. i don't care
if it's annie's birthday. food is food.
why 3 tins of abalone? dried scallop!
you take them back & get a refund.
mr song, at home, wants his wife
return some abalone, scallop
&, while he's going at it,
& while she's about it,
tins of longan, a large packet of mushrooms,
& these as well, this, that also lah
(& blah).

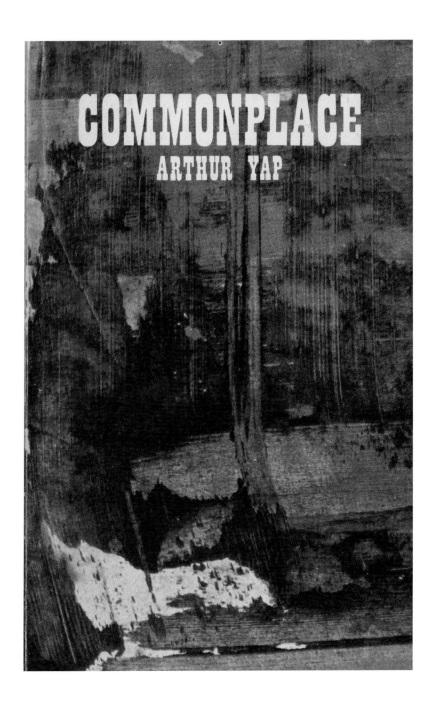

COMMONPLACE

1977

black & white

impact of collision. the long-legged road in convulsion.
2 school children, uniform-clad,
spread blue on the zebra-crossing. one, the other,
or both may not return from the brink.

a beautiful day. a new jaguar glides by.
all spectators shift focus: black & white to red,
draining into the spectrum of blood. 'must be at least
60 thousand'. 'who can afford such nonsense?'

black & white report. witnesses' testimonies.
respective heartaches. black & white dissolve
into grey. traditional chinese painters adduce 7 greys,
7 grey days a week. 7 dead zebras.

everything's coming up numbers

the death of the prime minister of china
left a wake of sorrow & a flock of numbers;
the death of the prime minister of malaysia
left a similar sorrow & a different set of numbers.
in market places, coffee shops,
the communal privacy of homes,
telephone & pencil were relaying numbers:
do we add 3 to his age?
put 6 at the end, or as the third digit?
do we follow the same for him as well?

the betting-booths displayed a list of numbers,
numbers already oversubscribed by collective certainty.
they were, therefore, not to be further abetted.
someone's death, it was felt, need not
incur one's corporate economic grief.

some bargirl's suicide. the old tree at the cemetery.
the wrecked mazda, the doubled-up honda,
their number-plates are shown in the papers clearly.
the little boy weaving between cars at the junction,
his mah-piew-poh may inform of remuneration.

everything's coming up numbers:
an old shoe with the manufacturer's code,
a child's first word at 2.30, wed., the 14 th.,
a film star's number of stab wounds.
somewhere, someone, so many times, what;
what, where, somehow, who says so;
what figures, where, add which, whom,
you saw what time, how many, good or not.

some friends

one of my friends has green fingers,
she grows grasshoppers quicker than flowers.

another, always wanting to get me a better job,
peruses the classified ads. avidly for his next stop.

another, once a staunch undergrad socialist,
now scoffs at all stupid, rash idealists.

another, pitying the starving millions of the third world,
merely prattles & even this world becomes a blurr.

another, a devout practising vegetarian,
eats eggs with a heap of chopped onion.

another, who celebrates each & every religious festivity,
has given all gods a rest & taken up other civilities.

i have yet to meet them all at once
for fear of the confusion that will arise:
civil eggs with chopped idealists,
grasshopper jobs with fringe-benefit onions,
ex-green-fingered socialists, floral vegetarians.
(o gawd, another friend's injunction)

dog-eared

the only really shabby people i know of
are the rich, or those who imagine themselves so.
but the saints all had long hair,
tattered clothes (though a halo, if icon-ed)
& it's difficult to draw the line
between the contemporary shabby
& those so in the past.

if we believe in reincarnation,
the only really shabby people i know of
are saints of the past but, then,
they won't be rich, or imagine themselves so.
when they step off a plane (or mainly out of line)
they seem to take their poverty so becomingly.
this pleases no one,
irritates some who would tend to them
with words, glances or scissors.
(but step out like birds with appended plumage:
an entire ballroom is taken to reenact their passage).

the nouveau pauvre do not live in kennels,
they sit in penthouses & fume a little
if they have been misinterpreted.
sometimes, filling in forms & coming to 'occupation',
they do not write 'x's reincarnation'
but, frequently, (such-or-such).
it is not their business to be otherwise
or to understand why they are apostatized.

on reading a current bestseller

the naming of parts, never direct,
is nevertheless carefully alluded to. the lovers,
anatomised, have their parts, if not their roles,
served up to the eye: proxy voyeur.
a paragraph's a huff,
a page a pant.
(who was it ran a mile under 4 minutes?)

who is the grammarian?
the naming of the parts (of speech):
today's lesson, refer your eyes
to page 11, prepositions —
in, up, between,
up & down,
in & out.

today's follow-up, page 92, botany:
rose, core, flowering,
an arboretum where all blooms boom.

some flights have been stretched without much sweat.
much sweat, sometimes, without skin.

inventory

under repair:
slums, broken hearts,
robbers & robbers inc.,
plastic lips, doctored orders,
jack the ripped,
laws of gravity, potted rainbows,
roof tiles, latent heat,
cumulus clouds, inert gases,
cultural bilges & misc. eruptions.

undergoing change:
all those above.
solid geometry, liquid water,
potential energy, woeful weals,
bad manners, decent exposure,
culture vultures & dovetail joints,
elementary humanities,
second-degree burns & culpables,
malleables, shapeables, feasibles, plausibles,
probables, liables, viables, possibles,
finger-printed sandwiches.

notice on wall, flanked by a calendar
& a cockroach or two:

All repairs are subject to alteration without
prior notification. All clients are respectfully
requested to redeem their gift repair coupons by
the first of every month, instant, for purposes
of compilation. All repairs become null & void
within 3 minutes.

miss lee 1940

miss lee opened her own front door.
in peacetime, she was half-tempted to explain,
there would have been a maid with a blush.

miss lee 1970.
vaguely, there is this thing called modernity,
the multiplicity of all hardship:
maids without blushes
(bold as you please),
maids without maid,
the cosmetic blush,
the blush-on face.

horrendous. (horrendous).
miss lee folds her arms
quietly behind her,
has had leapt over a japanese war,
shown two 1950 suitors to the door,
& now this, this.

next year
miss lee intends to learn origami
& fold baby tears in little nappies.

a circle

the kingfisher is said to fly so fast
it seems to be chasing after its own cries:
so the singer singing very loudly
appears to be chasing her own ears:
the deft tucks of the plastic surgeon
the former face is left in aberration:

somewhere
allthetime chasing:
the puppy after its tail,
the end after the beginning,
all sorts of ends for all sorts of means,
the crime to fit the punishment,
a Meaningful Arrangement of life
after a meaningful arrangement of fiction,
dry spasms for wet tears,
public grief for private traumas:
allthetime unending:

images unlimited:

dreams & reality pte. ltd.:

no directors, no operators:

all major & minor shareholders.

opening day

all this: oasis of carpet, drapes,
stainless steel, silvered tiles,
new uniform, polished counters,
italian furniture, monolithic chandeliers.

outside: a tall, slim hexagonal artefact
glints in the sun, seems to dissolve in rain,
foregrounds a stretch of s'pore river,
hoards up some airspace for birds.

floor by floor: instant plants,
carried out from lifts,
go on their own quiet ways
inhaling the first few batches
of balmy recycled air.
every corridor leads to every quiet hum.

especially this morning: early arrivals,
brisk greetings, timed chitchat/social cement,
a louder quiet hum.
the main doors quickly open:

the building seriously got down to business.

letter from a youth to his prospective employer

sir: i refer to my interview & your salary offer:
you said i would be given a commensurate salary:
commensurate with what? the depth of the filing
cabinet or the old bag sitting 3 desks & one right-
hand corner away? i am reasonably qualified:
quite handsome: my lack of experience compensated
by my prodigal intelligence: i shall not expect
to marry the typewriter: it's decision-making
i am after: that's what i am: a leader of tomorrow:
so why don't you make it today? my personality
is personable: & all opportunities being equal:
i am equal to any most opportune moment:
any most momentous opportunity: so take me
to your highest superior: & spare nothing:
at my earliest convenience: yours faithfully

prof

when he passed the quadrangle, there might
have been in him the desire to be a statue;
aloof from supposition or conjecture:
to be accessible to all,
whatever the weather,
at some plane beyond the clouds.
in the gloomy theatre, an immense face
composed of many insights,
prefacing a lecture with 'if & only if'.
if only we could care,
if only we could understand.
this we do learn, with his charisma,
prof m is entitled to recycle
bullshit as bullion.

still life: woman with birds at richmond

no one could, of course, mistake her
for a pigeon; the many flying about
do not mistake her for a tree, a large tidbit:
imperfect composition.

she sits in full sunlit river breeze
heavily sinking in her plastic bucket-chair,
pigeons fly at the command of her hand
-thrown bits of rock-bun the cafe sells
& hardly anybody ever eats.
whirr of wings, grey in harsh sunlight,
dazzlingly white in postcards.
the woman's stillness & toothy smile:
one composition.

north hill road, leeds

the few 11 pm lights are busy exchanging signals
with, above, the glinty stars:
little poke-holes on a large black tarpaulin
pegged down by nerveless wintry branches.
the frosty road raises itself up one hump
before dissolving in a flight of steps.

i'm already in my room
wallpapered with a few numbed thoughts;
all the books piled high on the shelf
make me think only of hot coffee.
looking out of the window, i see myself
walking up the road, down the steps:

this image i seem to see continually
as if it demands a profile
now that i'm no longer there.

new year 75, leeds

we wandered into a new year, as if by error.
at the chinese restaurant, my vietnamese friend & I,
the only asians, ordered 2 bowls of noodles.
the waiters served graces & teeming dishes
& the good laodiceans smiled warmly & scrutably.
our noodles finally arrived,
steaming under a turned-up nose.
vu's cossack-like cap still on his head,
my ears belonged once again to me in the warmth;
our cheer our tea, our leedsfraumilch 75,
kitchen-fresh vintage.

earlier, we had been to the plaza where x-rated films
are !ined up each week, cheek by jowl. no psychological
reality, vu's comment. i forget if i had a rejoinder.
leaving the resturant for our hostels, we passed
austicks, bookshop & frequent haven from the cold,
brotherton library, one side of woodhouse moor:
all somewhat remotely outlined in a thin swirling snow.
his hostel first, half a mile more for me:
everything behind were already soft-focal —
snow, steaming noodles, celluloid close-ups,
& night's myopia. next day, next year.

evening

bilabial at the edge of earth & water
stepping-stones like giant molars
grow old, grow dead.

under an aestival sun
daffodils have bloomed, dead
now, keening in a heap.

side-stepping these stones, people grow tired.
scattered images, mossed stones,
a fallen tree, annual rings felled:

sudden flare of an evening,
supposition of night blown by a slight breeze
right here, right now.

accelerando

so easily forgettable:
this baleful sky hangs like grey felt,
one rusty-toned star & defined silhouettes
of tall buildings nail in a large loom of despair.

slowly, with your umbrella,
you do not even talk of the weather.
rows of orange lamplight appear & dissolve,
move away to other eyes.
suddenly there is a screech of brakes,
or there isn't; a rude word in pedestrian collision.
swiftly, snowflakes are swirling down.
the sparkle of a little boy's eyes,
his brown mittens, sprinkled white,
are stretched out right into the sky.
the rusty-toned star drops out of sight.
the sky has swallowed the city
in one unforgettable gesture.

a patch of yellow cabbage flowers

none. at the supermarket, 12 p per cabbage
flowerless. late autumn already.
i want to say: this year's cold comes too early.
suddenly i have a desire to return home.

flux of ventilation in small puffs across the hall.
player's have gone up by 7 p.

nearby, at woodhouse moor,
gardeners dig up weeds in rented lots.
a patch of fading sunlight,
a patch of yellow cabbage flowers,
a patch of garden, cabbageless,
conjuring a juxtaposed pattern
of leaves, autumn's diary entries,
very real; today.

caernavon, wales

at noon, pausing at the turret,
the landscape below the castle
is rocked by the eyes.
the wind is sharp.
words seem to condense
at the tip of the nose
or, when released,
blown away directionally.
was it a bus missed,
a souvenir-shop scoffed at,
they come to rest?
or, way below the bridge, carried
by the swift-running water
(which seems to flow over jelly-knees)
they are given inadvertence, articulately?

a scene

the car eats scenery as it goes along.
in the car we eat sandwiches, coughdrops,
& into each other's nerves.
outside, bigger backdrop
darkening. at one spot
a large tree marvellously
bilocates night & day.
its trunk, tangentially at a seen distance,
beckons night to come in from one side.
meanwhile, day drains away from the other.

the last train

the last train to finchley
carries a deep-frozen chicken
that has been, at the festival hall,
parked for 3 hours;
2 for its owner to hear s. richter
playing his 'hammerklavier'
and I, for 2 coffees,
divided ½ & ½,
before recital & aft.

the last train to finchley
carries a deep-frozen chicken.
the thawing is at easter
after morning coffee & waffles,
disjointed at dinner.
the drumsticks are fake,
it never had legs.
the stuffing is sage,
soggy & polythene-fresh.

the last train to finchley
carries a discarded deep-frozen chicken
with 6 drumsticks,
2 for easter, 2 for x'mas,
2 tacked on for luck.
who belongs to the chicken
imported from holland?

it is said the cock
was never identified.

lunch-hour concert, leeds town hall

the drizzle of the piano fills not the hall.
in the rain, let your notes swim to us.
a spray of fingers rises & falls,
everything else still as a mask.

it is said you have 10 fingers plus one.
but they have grown fat, a soggy hotdog rap.
tight & clumsy, a spluttering bunch.
o a p's are quick to snatch a nap.

the drizzling rain drowns not the hall.
in the rain, a dying swimmer
swims to the piano, surfaces & then falls,
clutches at the lid, distributes the keys

in a, in b, sharp, flat. sudden fortissimo.
regaining, hair over flying fingers
describing & outlining a buoyant piano
with a stream of notes that lingers & lingers

a summer funfair

the stall-keeper calls out: candied apples,
& seems not at all to mind a mouthful of dust.
the man from the shooting-gallery
gazes at other stalls, all just as empty,
& walks carefully over uneven ground
for a chat & check with the owner
of the merry-go-round. he spins it intermittently:
children are few. for whatever reason
there are very few funfair bodies.
commercial travellers in transit, undergrads
preparing for an examination, are less likely
to materialize than that the magician,
billed as 'the great wiz' can pull lions
out of his trick-bottom top-hat.

in fading light, the field with its stalls, streamers,
& tents pale into gestalt stripes,
a factory of vague anxiety.
but, whatever it is,
with so many changes & resitings,
no passer-by would regard it
as merely a product coincidental to a practical scheme.

commonplace

daybreak. arms & legs.
breakfast. day lengthens: commonplace
situations & people. you say:
let's meet for lunch.

afternoon's 2 nd movement, andante,
as if groaning a bit.
everything has happened before
but there is nothing to compare it
each time, with each time that it recurs;
& i should never whip the commonplace
for the meaning of its opposite,
especially at daybreak, with blue
shadows to protract into a shadowless noon.
2 o'clock: 2 stained blobs on a clear canvas,
3 o'clock: 3 fingers tapping a tattoo on the table
are 3 upwind gulls, sliding, side to side,
wings hung out still. now and then a small shrug,
only to gather lift for this weaving, unweaving,
white & grey shuffle, as playing at cards,
writing a letter.
4 o'clock: like yesterday's glance,
still holds true. this morning's streets
are already rattling cars & buses back
into younger & less immediate parts of the city.
commonplace evening, the place is the same.
when night comes, it will come in neonlights.
when night comes, will it come in darkness
or will it bring its own light to a well-scrubbed day?
will there be doubt that commonplace is?

gaudy turnout

if i were you, i would walk the dark night
into some brightness, a lamp-post or lit shop-front,
& stop at the door. adjusting shoelace or smile
i wish i could find the doorsteps of the cellar-club,

the quick of your heart. how i wish i could
know for sure about tomorrow's party:
how many, who, won't be there. sensitive is the ear
of night & hears a loneliness for miles.

will there be dancing cheek-to-cheek? will someone
be recounting minutely his peculiar operation?
& is someone keeping score? will you
shut the door? why do you groan & groan?

if I were you, a gaudy boy afflicted with joy:
sensitive is the eye of day & sees a leer for miles.

& the tide

& the tide which is being urban-renewed
at bedok must go on its own tidy ways
without too much of a fuss,
coming in as riprap waves
met by the breakwaters
or going out sufficiently
for undisturbed analysis.
& the sum of their margin:
a littoral of slightly raised damp sand
& carefully arrayed litter.
out there where the waves curl,
the liquid is greenly uneven
in the sun's rays & the sky's
layers of noon darkness.
the renewal of a large imagination
may be rare, in a seascape.

there is no future in nostalgia

& certainly no nostalgia in the future of the past.
now, the corner cigarette-seller is gone, is perhaps dead.
no, definitely dead, he would not otherwise have gone.
he is replaced by a stamp-machine,
the old cook by a pressure-cooker,
the old trishaw-rider's stand by a fire hydrant,
the washer-woman by a spin-dryer

& it goes on
in various variations & permutations.
there is no future in nostalgia.

an afternoon nap

the ambitious mother across the road
is at it again. proclaiming her goodness
she beats the boy. shouting out his wrongs, with raps
she begins with his mediocre report-book grades.

she strikes chords for the afternoon piano lesson,
her voice stridently imitates 2 nd. lang. tuition,
all the while circling the cowering boy
in a manner apt for the most strenuous p.e. ploy.

swift are all her contorted movements,
ape for every need; no soft gradient
of a consonant-vowel figure, she lumbers
& shrieks, a hit for every 2 notes missed.

his tears are dear. each monday,
wednesday, friday, miss low & madam lim
appear & take away $90 from the kitty
leaving him an adagio, clause analysis, little
pocket-money.

the embittered boy across the road
is at it again. proclaiming his bewilderment
he yells at her. shouting out her wrongs, with tears
he begins with her expensive taste for education.

conceptual art

is enough.

when a picture is removed
the patch of wall it clung to
shows a contrasted freshness, exactly
the size of the picture.

the resulting afterimage,
to be sure, is precise,
is exact, is clear.
to be sure, it effloresces,
is out of tone with wall,
is, strangely, too loud.

is,
too, enough.

a figure study

dressed up to the eyes in fatigue,
arm in a sling or not in a sling:

this, the way he appears.
what cannot be committed to resolution
the sling can salve;
we can look, saying 'so it is'.
we hear some song & look for a radio,
we see an arm & hook it slung.

the coffee house, cockpit hotel

not a daily occurrence:
a bride waiting, 7.30 pm, at a coffee house.
you, shifting eyes, forkfuls into mouth,
stop. stop & watch the bride,
2 bridesmaids & an elderly chaperon
at the little round table
having a respite before the dinner.
her eyes, downcast, become modest behaviour.

immediately one floor down
dragon room is taken for the reception.
relatives line up at the entrance,
the men clutching proffered tins of rothmans.

twice, a hand gently steals out & pats
any suspected flaw of coiffure into perfection.
most of the time, looking at her gloves,
her eyes are downcast, cast downwards
one floor immediately below.

at the end of an elastic hour
will she rise, raise her eyes,
descend one floor, ascend the low platform
elevating the tabled 10 courses,
smile gently at the groom, post-sharksfin
& pre-crispy chicken & mark out clearly
her domain, right here & right up there?

quiescence

night is vital, its curved branch
shows signs of the morning
which grow & are little birds
singing ahead of the dawn,
wings panning violet clouds.
my hand cannot open the window
(because it is growing).

i'll wait for midday
to unfasten the bolt of dreams.
climbing up these stairs in creaks
the sun is taped on my shoulders
& with every step i take
i think this house is getting older.
windows are unfolding,
i can't keep my eyes on the dawn
(because it is evening).

landscapes

a few trees do not add up to a landscape:
the sparse foreground needs a few children
running & chasing each other. one or two
background isolates touch puffy clouds
& drain all attention away into vague blue.

seems strange,
this coeval terrain:
as if the sea is coming out tops,
white gulls, a few children running on sand,

on grass so green it's tinged with blue,
a few whitewashed huts.
& the children, if they are still running

running around the paucal,
the little plural, of landscapes.

similes

like one of those refined persons
who go out to scrub for the rich
because they cannot abide contact with the poor:

the canker to the rose.
but sunflowers also burst from dung
& fingers of unfortunates wring out tunes,
tall buildings on reclaimed land.

like one of those refined persons
who go out to loll about with the lazy
because they cannot abide contact with the orderly:

the garden reverts to jungle,
the go-slows become die-offs.
the ants & bees
of society lose their ability
to tidy up in the wake of faded levis.

dawn

dawn in the quiet key of light
utters a whole paragraph of hues
in the early mutter of an aviary.

clear upward lift of night,
tensile & then quickly certain:
the lively key to morning
is mysteriously sharp, already laden
with the still, angular mirrors of noon.

the day obtains itself.
the evening obtains skies & dawn.

absolute

morning is already late
in rounding the corner of living,
windowpanes of tiny raindrops
cling uncertainly, left from night rain.

strange you are asleep,
often waking so early
to see the leaves weave
skeins of cool air between trees
at the corner of these buildings.
i think i'll get this in a picture,
hang it on a nail
& set the sky within its frame.

seeing,
i shall dispel dimness.
& sorry if i should awaken you;
i've gathered morning like a flower,
it doesn't smell for me.
(i can tell by the cheer in your eyes
you've never quite learnt to believe).
later, & still later of the morning,
morning it is,
& absolutely nothing is wrong

who plots, then...

who plots, then, the words
talking, taking from the breath
the beat slow or fast?
among other things, a song
quick or slow: a testament
that is to be like a monotony.
give it form, certainty,
give it familiarity.
give it up.

afresh,
what it is are sounds
of the surroundings, near or far,
interweavings & interlacings
sounding, sounding

like what?

tones

still one-eared, a concentrated outpouring of
blurred recodes.
the listener remains peripheral to the monologue.
listening has always, if you will,
its hard-hearing edge.
the speaker is like every weather, structured in
rubrics:

a cool nebulous morning.
it is not the illusion of truth
nor the reality of falsity.
nothing is said, we are welcome
to what is not on parade.

a hot afternoon.
listening makes us careless.
scorching words on the ear
& our ears' quick-grasped replies:
the spitting & the swallowing,
as it were, in one gulp.
replying makes us careless.

a dark night:
tone hones tone.
when exasperated, darkness still operates
in residue. a curfew on direct speech.
reporting makes us careful,
trading performatives for passives.
listening makes us deaf.
deafness has always, if you will, no hard-hearing aid.

another look

About suffering they were never wrong,
The Old Masters: how well they understood
Its human position.
    — W. H. Auden, *Musée de Beaux Arts*

how an adaptation
between canvas & the hand:
an old masterly breath
dispensed sectorial suffering.
here, where it all is going on
is not the locus; but further
up or down are the spatial reactions
for surprise or sadness.
never level, the locus, this suffering
has to be watched carefully.
the stabbed figure in convulsion
has a destiny to go into,
an explanation, an appraisal,
a catalogue-listing.

never level, this suffering, this locus:
what it is, the literal size
incorporates, & larger or smaller
than life, this resinous suffering,
less frenetic, keeps pace
with or without contemporaneous occurrence.

dracula

an eye-mixture of the modern & the past,
of the practical & the fancifully wild
(compounding channel 5 news with channel 8 fiction)
dracula's extravagant features melted
a pair of frightened but beautiful eyes,
her flushed & his comic face, so intent on badness,
i could not see him in the role of fiend.

a very wet &, as it seemed to me, transfigured stare,
an angry red puncture on her noughts & crosses throat.
on her throat there was that angry red tincture.
drac put his immortal hand to his stupid forehead,
& a cry in which joy & rehearsal seemed blended.
it was a recall associated with the giant bat
from hades, 2 man-eating spiders, 7
9-children eating frogs,
a sequel for which the world is tomorrow fully prepared.

things

chair
wall
window
desk
bed

chair makes us fat, upholstered in blubber.
long shot: wall. no one has ever succeeded
in being hung up like a portrait, truly dead.
medium shot: window. open it.
let the sun in, let suicide out.
before hitting the ground, frame it in slow motion.
reverse repeat, pan it back to window, its source.

to think up such imperfect realia
i'm at desk. it isn't true that one dreams in bed.

configuration

anything is better than stagnation,
the world seems big & kind enough to all;
a hongkong lady, daughter of a merchant
he had met in connection with the trading of jade.
the lady, very pretty,
began to show some curious traits,
quite alien to her usual sweet disposition,
to a charming & affectionate youth
unhappily injured, being shot at
in connection with the jade trade.
day & night the jade lady covered the youth
with prayers &, then silent, like an alert nurse
stayed in wait in case the child stirred.
his frame had fallen in,
his eyes were vacant.

(but the most loving heart within)
it seemed a childhood fall & a twisted spine
now righted, & her father's wealth, the lady
became celebrated. over his bowed shoulders
she laid her hands as if in benediction.
his wan looks like pale jade
which is life & death to her,
a physical puzzle to the doctor.
it is certainly delicate, said the man
who met her father in connection with jade.
up to now i've not been struck by its simplicity

hibiscus

these crunchy-looking orchids are like salad
vegetables. a gardener goes round each day,
sprays, keeps nasty insects away.

(there'll never be a craze for hibiscus)

sturdy orchids outlive their owners,
own their owners very completely
by hook, pot & crock,
own all their own roots & arms,
own dignitaries by their names
& are very hung up about their ownership.

(there'll never be a craze for hibiscus)

this year's new hybrid is gold,
a plastic box protects it from tacky fingers.
hibiscus are left to insects & new ownership
by reclaimed hedge. a floral transfer is minted.

1–2 min. poem

the riders on motorbikes are not carefree,
at red lights talk busily on crucialities
interspersed with laughter to make them less heavy.
turn on the throttles:
& this racial 'thing' becomes a real bother,
why are there so many bloody stupid people?
readjust helmet straps:
& the carnival that has just ended
becomes a real farce, though damn well attended
the organizers should be shot.
blink an eye-lid:
& the freshies & the oldies
are seen in their colours truly
(but not related to this social 'thing').
no issue of this little world
escapes a summarized good or evil,
there's precious little time
so with this onus on their pillions
& assignments incomplete
(no time, you know, no time)
they roar.

merdeka highway
opens swiftly, strongly,
to receive these divinities
unwaveringly sure
in their 1–2 minute destiny.

group dynamics i

first, it was steamed eyes when the soup arrived.
eyes clear, glasses demisted, next the steamed fish stared.
was it for these we were there? dead pieties.

a speech after dinner, barer than the walls.
figures of speech of elation & ramification
didn't help. empty pieties.
dessert after dinner, longans & words.
a bit of leg-stretching, (not too much),
mustn't be seen with socks not pulled up.

elastic pieties, expandable by the hour,
relaxed conditionals:
if & then only if we weren't there,
if & then only if (unreal condition) the speech
weren't there, the speaker weren't there.
then, the soup wouldn't have,
the fish shouldn't.
& what's there left?
in absentia. in praesentia, weren't
                                    much

group dynamics ii

reginald is 19, very smart & somewhat bored.
wingho is like reginald, without the honda sports.
benny is like wingho, both are wong.
may-lin comes from another school
& our pre.u's real strong, you know.

wingho calls may-lin sis & she giggles.
julie, also wong, thinks it's all so wrong
all this giggling, & i don't always want to go out.
she does if they are, (ring-ring) she's in, julie speaking.

let's chase them. reginald sped. stupid nut
may-lin said. stupid nut wingho said
to any driver reginald had overtaken.
to bedok julie said. go to bedok, you bodoh
wingho said. we'll send you a postcard, julie
indicated, forming an oblong with her fingers.
swiftly passed-by drivers registered no surprise.

next week let's go....
(a screech) simultaneously almost
the lampost quivered forward. thrown forward, julie
reached out as if to light it. reginald's face
wiped the sole of wingho's shoe. the windscreen wove
a spider's web. the mascot on may-lin's lap.

reginald's licence is suspended.
julie still sulks. may-lin doesn't worry,
she's going to university.
never mind what faculty
she puts the phone down on benny.
wingho is like reginald,
benny is like wingho.
they wait for the bus,
they wait for a taxi
to take susie & bee ngah
to the troika.
they wait for the call-up.

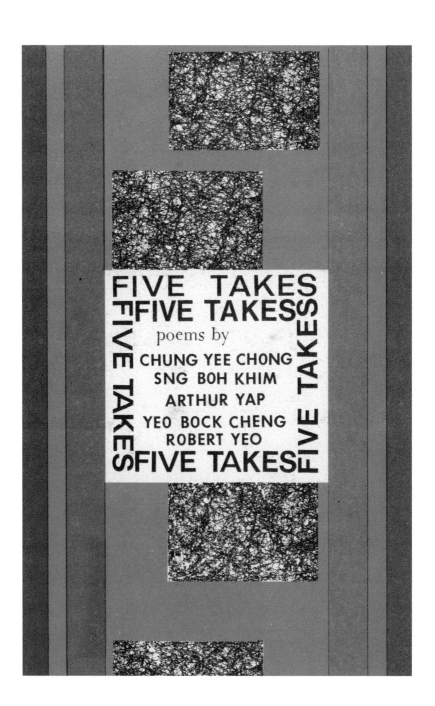

FIVE TAKES
1974

dramatis personnae

i. public park

along the bench we're variations of a line
that watch the many flowers grow
into our understanding, and die
because we are not to pick them.
they are for the public,
we in public are private figures
humanising the landscape
on the little hill. under the trees
we listen for the millennium
while following the turn of the floral clock
with the knock of a new plastic heart.
this park is self-centred
it takes and it rejects.

this park is self-centred
and outsiders just get in the way.
today you are in the park
waiting for us, watching us
young men and women, old boys and girls,
parking ourselves. (how we laugh).
how we laugh and then cry,
since we bring you some happiness
you should also have some of our sadness

ii. public beach

where does the road end and the beach begin?
it is not easy to say, so closely
do the two forms intermingle
blending the neat sharp smell of petrol
with the warm scent of dirty sand

here is the sand,
and further from the sand
(can you see?)
here is the sea.
sand and sea are less today
as there is more of life

webbed up here by the sewer
sewn to the hardness of cement
trapped by piss-moss, little landcrabs
are more crust than crab and salt.
and caught here, we would never have been
more than all these things we have seen.
that cemented here, as we are not,
we run away before the waves arrive
with a little last fresh collapse

iii. public pond

coming down to the very bank
the soil is very old and crumbly.
you would not laugh
seeing it so, for it is yours.
today you are a pond, a still pond
hoping for the little boys to happen
there with their jars, here with their nets.
they drown
because you are too abstract
when they bend over you
searching among weeds for what they want
before they turn to conceits, the lesson
on fish and waterlife and diagrams,
with no waterdrops of agitation on their hands

it is important they come each sunday
replacing the week's gloom with their faces.
in you they drown, an old familarity,
and they will rise again day after day
after this, like some terrible fish.
for their simplicity is your certainty

the performance

as if it were not already bad enough
the crowd had to jeer, (no one cheered).
and all you wanted to do was quibble.
whether the performance was that poor.

as if he didn't know any better
he would start singing for himself,
not for the rest of the room.
some anxiety was pulling away his song,
his face, his hands, his feet,
all of which were also singing
a different desperate song
(perhaps of running away);

so let him fall, kick into a silence.
water him with roses and nightingales,
images of pursuing faces, left-over beer.
then, as if he were going to rise,
cry or be enraged; pull off his shoes,
laugh, swagger a little and sing for peace

parochial champion

when you have painted yourself into a corner
and there's no way out except by leaving a trail
of prints, wetly breaking the surface of the floor:

think sometimes of yourself as a parochial champion
who is editing the footprints systematically,
pointing out a path where others
(ideally they should just come and go)
can tread and all directions become just one.

you may not know what lie below:
words, lies, puns, people from downstairs.
so go as you lead and follow your own safe path
making each step a comment, manifest
for censorship or any other -ship
or carry, since you have the strength,
cultural ethos, socio-economic problems, with wisdom
of the years to come when what use are these prints
which after all are broken patches of varnish-skin?

look instead with ease at the shiny new escalator
which moves unmysteriously also in one direction
and that is: up and up and up

statement

of course your work comes first.
after that, you may go for a walk,
visit friends but, all the same,
it is always correct to ask
before you do anything else.

so if you say: please may i jump
off the ledge? and go on to add
this work is really killing,
you will be told: start jumping.
no one is in any way
narrow-minded anymore these days.
it is that everyone likes to know
these things way beforehand.
but if you state: i'm going now,
jumping off the ledge
most probably they will say nothing,
thinking should it legally, morally,
departmentally be yes/no/perhaps,
or if it's not too late:
why don't you come along? we shall bring
this matter up to a higher level

fire off kim seng bridge

a burning sun
as i watch
clatters on the bridge

scattering black butterflies in the breeze.
burning huts throw pale flames in the heat.
drawing so much anodic space
huts and people seem to nudge
towards the centre of the heap.
smoke seams the scene
in a sheet of silence.

and so what are world crises,
spearheads of unrest so prevalent?
in this silent fear
the rest becomes conditional,
and things being coeval
you could walk out and get killed.
it makes so little difference

the send-off

even as children are chanting fascinations
about new year, we mythologise the act and fact
of its passing. passing, the opening of the year
wears its traditional accessories, with red
to balance in the ecology of superstition.

the year that is past
substituted its time and movement for yours
and took you away from nothing
not already familiar, asked nothing
not already dispensible.
a year has no revelations,
it must come and go
making some older, some younger by their absence.
a year conceals, does not reveal
meanings, portents or omens.
it springs with the tiger, sneaks in with the rat
and if it is not wet, a dry year cherishes itself
sunning the tower-block and the hut.
old griefs, new hopes
all become their own revelations
as the city sleeps, is tired from the weight
of responsibility that is time's endowment

these sounds, endlessly

these sounds, endlessly. ears were had.
it wouldn't have been bad had they
been of leaves falling. instead, they were many things
going away: harsh grating removal noises
incessantly, heaving the house inside out.

inside out,
the new house is a few new sounds.
when these fail, ears are had.
it is sad to add that when ears fail
eyes are also had
by a little graphic failure
(true to scale,
very dear
the ways things go).

going, feet are gone.
so let there be not too much hurry,
there is nothing that does not need move
away. any way
you see it
you are there, had, (too bad).

almost still-life

it was easy to become a stranger.
having walked into every room,
all rooms were empty.
i wondered if what troubled me

was not this house, this old man
whose window-ears have been constantly washed
by laughter and shouts of anger;
whose tattered shutter-eyes
(both precise and obscured)
have focused upon a paradox
and drawn it right up to the knees, its stairs,
so as not to show its heart empty.

the old house was like a shell
and seemed to have wrapped
emptiness up as a parcel.
i could not see its eyes clearly
enough to know if, at midnight, the ghosts
would come and retrieve the gifts
of bricks and concrete and fingers

recurrent imagery

just as the tree which seems caught
a little ahead of an idiomatic sunrise
is but an image,
so is the student reading his thoughts into a book,
the painter and his paints,
and the woman nursing her newborn child
who looks like a little old man.

sun rising, the tree is not the same.
the child is fresh and fairly recent.
and every few years bring on differences
which, differently asked and answered,
are conceit to conceit
variously the same.

you do not think these are images.
sun and child start all over again
watching you watch them take away
colours from the face which had been yours,
and all you need is bring the tree to sun
itself in the corridor you have lined with your years

ARTHUR YAP

look beyond

that you have looked beyond yourself
does not imply there is another person,
my hedonistic friend.

that last night you were a tree
splintering new branches.
that today i have gathered you
as a botanical statement:
it is neither true nor false.
but if you are false
then day sweeps away the art,
not the guilt
that, somehow, things could be better

oyster-like

morning also resembles you
like an open translucent oyster
on the table, a few drops of sunshine
to balance the delicate complications.
you have a solution for the situation.

and have you some other solution
for such another clear morning
you may meet?

slowly.

if you haven't,
morning is already over.
you don't wear your lemon sun

clearly

186

minimum excavation

poised like a large settlement
of raw minerals at ground level
they are also for excavation,
these feelings of uncertainty.
pared to a minimum
the answer is
yes or no.

no intricate adornment
of fernroots, young shoots,
detract the hard and cold.
busy hands shift terrains,
lay down a horizon
dividing nothing
more than itself

which is finite enough in its suggestion
that long-ago memories
are now exposed, posing
for the benefit of stony spectators

people who now to us

people who now to us are familiar
fade soon into the shadows
where all, unknown, begin.
we might as well begin now
wrapping those images of a dream
which refuse conciliatory awareness
of the sun and travel
with a load of such dreams
on a constant road.

we do not.

the road we have not travelled
comes to us, lengthening and stretching
with introspection and prohibitions
we have or have not imposed, lifted;

and in personal and arbitary ways
their transformation into act begins

portrait

(why) when everything is quiet
there is still this sadness
imitation almost of joy
near you.

you have not changed
the way you look
with faded yellow flowers
in the picture.

the way you look
with faded yellow flowers
calls up again
bright yellow flowers
blossoming. and almost aerial
are you and your eyes,

now imitation of a more casual style

iteration

this is the dead of night.
many things alive
are sounds quiet and sad
droning on the ears
in just a whisper. your mouth
is an insect,
a nightbird on the prowl.

everything is the same
heart roving
quiet and droning,
another day
you are yourself. changing,
your lips change the refrain

banyan tree

showers catching the intersect
of this road and the next
grow the tree greener than paint.
its roots though themselves nothing
siphon in spreading air
pluck birds from the sky
to rest within its branches
which are many and many

and as they are not more specific
they loom, vague and impending.
bunched by breeze they move the hours
this way and that on a hot day.
encircled by a ring of streetlamps
this is a petrified monument.
starting here and ending there, it forms
an outline of the still and writhing.

then to see it next day,
its hands, large in the air.
applaud like loose thoughts
up and down the rigid landscape

a vague lesson of fear

the child runs.
it does not matter
nobody watches.
he runs concurrent
to somebody's question.

why are you running?
is not asked
to impede the speed
of your running feet.
right across where
another child is,
it is to arrest your heart.
he distributes larger footsteps,
stamps neater prints
over all the empty corridor.

you may hear
from outside the echoes
a quick footfall: tell all, tell all

unfinished letter

the note was brief and the house quiet,
the reader read the message out and was quick
to refuse every word, bouncing the lot
out of his world-wide window, which was dark.

the sky was an even, intense purple-blue,
flecks of orange and bad temper here and there.

excuse me, the reader said, while i go and slit
my throat. but write to me again,
this time write and confess fully
in words that are hard as nails
soft as the night really is

night scene

we stopped to smell the night.
just when the breeze served up dinner
odours, the road drank some rain
in uneven gulps. every smell faded.

the pavement looked distorted,
the litter stuck in the gutter.
tomorrow someone will grumble
at walk to work, even that will pass
and moments become silent,
objects will speak objectively

june morning

june morning,
the tiles on the roof do not look like wounds.
no wind has yet blown a heap of words
behind all these dusty books.

so that's something already. at other times
telling ourselves things aren't like that anyway
we like the scenery: branches over roof,
a little bird or two on the branches.
on the tabletop the wind
blows up a bouquet of tiny alarms
scattering a glass and some empty smiles.

think sharp:
this scene is also very brittle,
copes with the problem of the accidental
to make it come more fully to life.
you look up from your thick black diary,
frowning, lines fragile as little bones

and it is you who structure this scenery

mainly afterwards

the sun was lost in his view.
as if it had something new for the old earth
darkness fell quickly in all the country.
there at dungun, south china sea
ran over the lip of shore in heavy floods
and then floated a weak sunrise in a sea of mud

the whole of which was his,

this fisherman, standing in the flood.
he had felt the wind blowing his hair
rearing and stretching, like a marsh plant,
beyond his head. the wind is gone
and sea is secret with sun in the sky.
the fisherman useless, from the corner of his eye
the land fastens under the harsh waters

nature is merciless

nature is merciless.
a line must be drawn somewhere
between dark skies and leaky roofs:
between the dark sky and the leaky roof
is outlined for the retina
a little crushed melodrama.

if the alarm-mechanism of reason
fails not in this paroxysm,
nature is kind:
causes a similar reaction
in this room. one bulb
entices many flying ants.

a line must be drawn somewhere
between wings and the bright patina
before all dissolve into wind,
all colours run into black
and everything piles up
as wings beneath the light.
wing-abandoned ants crawl
after their wingless young.
it appears everything is older than before

open road

breasting a tall crest of road
the sky looms. quick capricious illusion
pushes away two banks of rubber trees.
this looming sudden expanse
gathers itself like a sullen face
which over the plantation breaks,
unfurling tight-curled tips of the topmost leaves
with slip-drops of water falling, scattering
lean dogs with humpy shivers.

only the cyclist's heart
halts at the sightless road, wet with eyes.
wet with life, the plantation is its difference
from dry days, definable days
of heat and light lallang seeds.
while the grass usually sizzles with blade-rubs
it now bends green arches under an uncertain rainbow,

the road slices through two lives
which are the quick and, mainly, the quicker

evening

one thing to mark is lovely:
see the weight of sunset
perch convergent on the horizon
washed by tide culled from here

seagulls rising
are erased by an arc of light
refracting direction of wings,
water out-folding
seals the earth beneath
and throbs over a mile of wind

town centre

waking early
the nerve-knotted resident
hurries
cars past lengthy tarmac arms
pedestrians across its ribs
and wears a wide grin of buildings

internationalism

it was after his luggage was stolen
(but his passport returned)
and social escort mabel
dropped his duty-free camera
out of the trishaw
taking them from an exotic dinner
(which wasn't)
that he learnt it was a lesson
on internationalism.

tanah rata

I

look how this slope is paved
with yellow cosmos
nodding to butterflies

and alike to passers-by
like us returning from brinchang
followed by five o'clock
sun behind us,
look how the slope ends with grass
flanking blown cannas

to which we can add
the old woman weeding
nodding to flowers
gradually growing upwards
and ending where the slope begins

II

missing a step
the path crazily laid
with broken bricks
fallen casurina leaves
and pockets of cold air

the child gathers himself up
to an unexpected smack,
his mother trundles on ahead
with a laden basket
lifts the latch of the gate
at the top of the path
turns back to the reluctant child
hauls him up with quick words

lays out vegetables
throws away wrapping paper
and lifting the child
kisses him, asks if he's hurt

battersea park, london

wintry branches reflected in water
are more clearly etched than the actual
in a classical collapse of the grey sky.
everything is growing downwards.
these, and these many acres of undiluted melancholy

are winter landscape, a free mind,
a free mind that throws everything
whether roaming or hibernating
at random into a picture.
my gloved hand bunched over a cigarette
is a strange little animal with a filtered tail.
i move, and it moves
leaving a little puff of trail.
in the frozen pond, upside down ducks
are other bits of surrealistic nonsense,

the madness of the season.
winter
the landscape cheats roundthecorner.

i am here because
where are you?

episodic

take away the heroes and villains
we are left with ourselves,
a book or a letter, and almost
definitely a third probability.

today, or even a while age,
i was eating breakfast. it was you.
right now, even right now
j'm writing this, it is late.

late.

your condition precedes any impression
i could have,
and because the condition precedes
this impression, i could have
(how strange) felt strange.

wintry morning outside.
this morning i think in spidery images.
when they are gone
you will come still closer

2 small songs

song of the wise mother:
child, now that you go to school
you will learn the sum difference
between a teacher and a blackboard
and the value of paper.
come to think of it, there is nothing
you cannot teach yourself
and succeed, without acknowledgement
thereof —

song of the mad mother:
child, now that you are no longer
part of me, i regret all i have
given you. but so much that it was
hand some over to the next

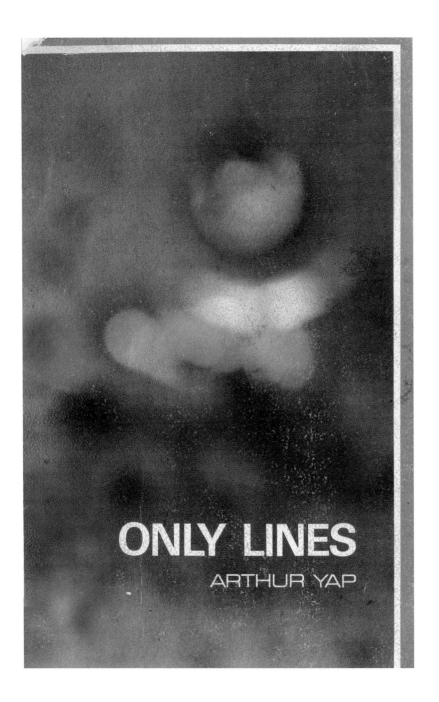

ONLY LINES
1971

only lines

should i also add:
here are only lines
linked by the same old story.
the same basic plot
in which they are grown

should add
little doubt the field is only green
the sky the same old blue
in the presence of my eyes,
your preference
(though not mine)
should see for your own eyes
and if you can laugh
care with some concern
it is because (like me)
you need lines
to add up this same old story

location

so this village is still here
here without change
and if i stay here any longer
i am already
where i shall always be
here without change

in this village still here.
some things remain
some things pass,
some things are tired
bicycles arriving
cleaned bicycles departing.
and if today
not many people are arriving
do not change the day
to bring in yesterday
riding an old identity
which, anywhere,
has come and gone
every year ago.
and if you see a bicycle
leaning on the grass
neither tired nor cleaned
then it is just resting
sufficiently
to make no sense at all

sunny day

sunny day
comes through the window
and sits on the table.

sunny day,
he chose to be killed
diaphragm against steering wheel
for the car seemed newer
the senses keener.
only the road was closer.

sunny day licks up paint
on the window-sill
and the heart, grown cooler,
(only the skin is warmer)
sees withering flowers
offered to him on the hill

and it is isolation

hurrying ahead

there was a large house up the road.
it is a small house
and mainly dead,
those living are moving out.

the road is like a snake
running a slow quarter mile,
needs shaping round the bend
to drain the rain easily.
the grass is past green
when a drought is on,
those leaving have to hurry
before the grass returns
to green for an eternity
and reality becomes more mixed
than is imagined.
then it is not so bad
for another eternity.
those moving are not just going
they are hurrying ahead
when the grass is dying
before they are also dying
dying a few steps after the grass
where they had come to live
not die
nor ask
why any grass should die

one road

the road northwards
ended at cha'ah
on a fine april morning,
here the car broke down
and the sun followed us
in a bus to segamat.

next morning
the road continued
under a repaired car.
glad were we to feel the breeze
hear the roar of other engines,
having ended a night's hotel discomfort
here were both open road
and prospect of city:
the sum of what's not small town.
it was here, at gemas,
it was here at tampin
we wondered if we hadn't passed
this way yesterday
for at any four o'clock
children were pyjama-clad.

if we can be sure
that the road running hundreds of miles
would not bring along its periphery,
that here and there
when it is twelve o'clock
the sun has not risen nor set

then everything else could well wait

panchor

year by year
wood returns to ashes
and also as trees and flowers.
some grow some bloom
some wither and some rally
in support of others
as they climb and climb
to reach for the sun
splintering its light on the ground
touching the soil with life,
flow up as sap
bursting in green leaves
on branches of the wild rambutan.

squat under, the sultan's monument
is seen and appraised.
hands reached out
spanning the years
to pluck the rambutans
the sultan had never eaten,
throw the shells down river
where there was a ton of gold.

a little later
the boat pulled from the jetty,
there was a lull
and then the landscape settled down.

preparedly

you talk of precincts ways
bungalows terraces compounds,
i talk of complexes
(no, not that sort)
and duplexes:
now-residential nouns.

preparedly
you have open spaces
sunshine fresh-air
and children's balloons

i haven't a coda to your existence.

you have a situation
i have a problem:
so it looks like
(as if) we've equality.
you offered me lodging,
preparedly
it looks like
i've got equality
which, still mine,

fades like a road
which hurries me past
a situation
i don't know, which
is yours

a loud silence

its roar is momentarily
locked in the room
momentarily silencing the speaker,
mouth opened (to give
the marvellous roar)

and the plane made also
rue of comedy
of what was left
because little was left.
little more than words
little more than sense
little more than silence splintering
large in the wake
of the roaring break.
it's a pity
that the only part of a plane
which cannot be bought or sold
is the roar

new year

rarely
is it for the sun
to die its postercolour death,
daily

you entertain
your postercolour guests.
i just came along
you asked me, i didn't mind
looking at a sunset or sunrise,
if you've turned off the sun
at neonlights.
it didn't matter.
say it wasn't a parochial sunset
old as earth
say it was a day's old
young as grass (or anybody),
a sartorial sunset
cut and patched
as a bequest
      that
this year has begun again, you see,
and we didn't even have fireworks
          for last year's sunset

# of anything that is past

this death seems to have no name.
but it rules
to focus all inquiry
in all manners of things,
after all, what is beethoven picasso
moontravel me polaris you
or anything
when everything will pass.
we learn not to sit in the dark
in the dark with a past
past current care.
so shun this death
he's a million years old
he died yesterday
and took a lot of truth
out of the world with him

so until everyone dies
his descendents cannot
bear much sorrow or longevity

garden episode

in the garden two children
set fire to their sparklers
and it wasn't a festival.
the boy drew a coloured circle
showing the amah in the dark
perched on a little stool
and she was here a long time ago.
jubilant, the little girl's brand
trailed over a bush
with a shatter of light
quickly over
as they walked to the house:
"you're a big boy now, too heavy to carry".
she stooped over the puny child, barely five,
lifting him from under the arms
and trotted, fat, with the neglected girl
clinging to her samfoo.
her smile was like that, thirty years back,
of a slim woman vacant over a dead child;

while pulling each gently by the ear
to their bedtime, she had forgotten
that a few more years would make her
think of the night with little stars
as she grows punitive over two children
not weary from sums and rounders
scattering her thoughts freely as they come

expansion

no stretch of darkened sky
would show a patch of red
a patch of sunset.

where the sun will not stay
after dark
the skyline of houses
grows with the sky
and who can tell
what is this completion;
i cannot chew the month to days
masticate the day to hours
and line the hours each to each
saying, out of context, i die.
where once a single day
was a day and a night
it is now the amoeba of day
of night,
the line of sponge houses
soaks in the sky
as the sponge sky
seeps into the houses.
where once houses hung from sky
they now are clutches.
so one urban expansion
has to lean on another
or they die

while the tree of night grows and grows

news

it is already announced
today will be one to remember.

had to laugh today

saw your face neatly
reading from the screen,
the feeling is the same
as in all the other days
which were (also) ones to remember.

had to eat today

your words:
here's your news report
i'm your straight face for today,
sorry if it's short
i've to get away
and be very busy,

and the weather's hot.

i'm deceived by what i fear
by words i've yet to hear
by the news that's over
and the words which scuttle
after. after this, bring on
words which do not kill the ear

because

because saturday morning
we wear smiles
each large enough
to line up three faces

it's a boring discussion.
because boredom
curiously completes isolation,
it is saturday's assumed eccentricity
we are like spastic sparrows.
because we've found the grain
we feel (also) the strain
and disguise the pain with a song
of aggressive vociferation.

because saturday morning
we don't wear smiles
each large enough
for half a face,
we think we do
because our smiles
our faces otherwise
would be very null and very void
on all the other days
coming up, flowers

coming up, flowers.

coming up, flowers
and just how long
will it take to have all re-arranged?

fields sprawl in midday sun,
i must've been mad
to think i could live
with bricks and concrete
when, all the while,
the rurality pitched over
all its dung
wearing fields like badges.
growing flowers in batches
was the only bunch
of brickbats i've had.

flowers change with the months,
i wonder when it's my turn
to receive (your accolades)
but there's still the problem
of what happens when they're dead

perpetual

sit and watch this woman
in every house she hangs
curtains in every room,
takes out a pile of washing
to spread dry on every line.
every nearby baby perking in the sun
turns sweaty, cries hopefully
for another cake, another nipple.
every woman shouts in anger
does not anyway always whisper

does not at all read the papers
cares not for the moon's soft light
that erases every baby in sleep.
and every woman now is stalking
through all the days following

old photographs

mainly, they're old photographs,
my standing here, your standing there.

when my sister wrote from london
of hippies loitering along the streets
i've also seen them everywhere,
in Life and Time they appear
and it's difficult to tell if they loiter.

i must've seen in the flesh
people in memorable situations
either of success or failure,
only it cannot be claimed
such images are perpetual.
in newspapers they're more real
more decisive in their happiness or sorrow.

and, there, they're the oldest photographs.
it is that on one has changed

precedence

well into november, there hasn't been
the start of the monsoon.
voices have not preceded owners
helping themselves over puddles.
in a few days, likely
the sky will tremble with stored storms
that seen across the window will be
rain hanging over the road, not gentle
nor grating. it is a constant seeping
and a wind pushes it to new shapes
of landscape.

this evening it is raining stars
all the more clearly,
there is no spangling moon

it rains today

the trees are wet with rain today
a child holds an umbrella
walking over grass.
very quickly
a wind lifts his umbrella
the child is wet with rain today,

the trees in front of him
exist for every rain
and every rain
outside my window
comes before my gaze,
becomes this familiarity.
i always see.
rain after rain
until this rain
i've never found
trees child and rain
so precisely
a little shift
either side of reality

take a room

take a room with neonlights
outside
(and they're) comforting
mrs lee 500 yards ago
at the nightmarket,
now clipping her toenails

and 5 yards of balcony
open to her
60 feet below
lie the toenails.
these neonlights (are telling):
show mrs lee
now counting her marketing money
things go better with shell.

you who have been with her
night after night
never did see her (much)
because of the neonsign
over that restaurant
whose chiefcook-owner
mrs lee waxes
her vegetarian influence over

and over to you again, mr lee,
really quite old
your meal has been laid
(for you)
60 feet below

old house at ang siang hill

an unusual house this is
dreams are here before you sleep
tread softly
into the three-storeyed gloom
sit gently
on the straits-born furniture
imported from china
speak quietly
to the contemporary occupants

they are not afraid of you
waiting for you to go
before they dislocate your intentions
so what if this is
your grandfather's house
his ghost doesn't live here anymore
your family past is
superannuated grime
which increases with time
otherwise nothing adds or subtracts
the bricks and tiles
until re-development
which will greatly change
this house-that-was
dozens like it along the street
the next and the next as well

nothing much will be missed
eyes not tradition tell you this

in passing

yesterday you were at k.l., the day before you
were somewhere else; now, you are here
trying out our telephone-lines and the air-
conditioning system, saying that our system is
more adequate than that in new york where you
come from. but you are so tired of running and we,
not having run, drove you to the seaside restaurant
feted you on the speciality of chilli-crabs and fried
noodles to which you said: it's so unlike the
spaghetti i had in italy.

you brought, from a friend, an l.p. for us to share
with regards. you exclaimed in chinatown that it
was all so intriguing while we, not wanting to
be perfunctory, left you to your intrigue. then
at the airport, with its mural, its coffee, we
waited, while talking and talking, for you to comment
on the fine building, the mural assembling the sea-
front or, even, the air-conditioning.

but you were fumbling your bag for your sweater

domestic life

the place in question runs up a hill
not tall, a real-estate breezy hill.
that it has done so for a long time
is soon enough for some occupants
to move a few feet down
where the supermarket stands
and main road so close at hand
it noses the garden fence.

then the two houses were joined
one higher, adjacent to the other.
going up
coming down
they're the same,
a question only of direction
confused by a sheet of rain
on wet days.

then it's a question only of years
a shelter will span the two houses:
in-law communication
a new garage
give and take a few pot-plants
the unit is self-contained,
it's only sad
when the asphalt is slippery
the poor amah sustains a knee injury
(it's only wrong
when someone dies)

quick waltz (in may)

that may, it was also another day
another day for dying, for living
is less easy and no substitute
for a metaphysical bravery

unless it is another's dying.
so you died, taking away
much unshed tears and anger
just as the sun
sank into the sea
(like you now) it is daily
a heavyweight affair, quickly
everything was localized
by the electricity of bright lights
and bright lights, also more shadowy,
turn round the bed
where life has turned you down
leaving yourself with yourself

all your yesterdays merged
with all your tomorrows
and the present leaves you
with no point of view
on why you have died

10th floor song

(i imagine that) as the eagle
swoops into its eyrie
so do i, lifted up 10 floors;
the veneer crunch of a door

on the world outside, sun
with cuscaden house at the corner
and raffles village pausing in time
before its evening historical pageant
(seldom laid on for us).
i know this all already
no need to jettison our door

whatever pilferer you were at x'mas
(thinking all souls out-of-doors),
no need to bring the ambulance
to the porch
(whoever she was)
left leg over first floor ledge
was quite dead.

she went swimming only yesterday:
someone said, proof enough she was
alive before she is dead.
just a few miles away
the sea takes its ebb and tide,
this is the tall shore of urban rehearsal
and the flow is old enough
as it is (almost) everyday's

twin-point

but that is not the point:

it is well executed
this foreign woman, painted
roughly to look violated
(so it means) you know what
you can do with her

so she has been pummeled
and much· battered, an angry red X
added on her spread of thighs
so it means (afterwards)
she is colourfully censored.

the point is the painter's anger
has only killed a foreign woman
in his leisure, in all goodness
painterly protest brings the bread
so it means he got a grant
to tour that foreign country,
3 years he stayed
and only much farted

a recurrent event

in sago lane the cruellest scenes
can be seen — a dead relative
rises from the bed to undie
another year in his martyred home.
or an aunt in shroud
wonders if the last rites
would be performed suitably,
whether one or more monks
might chant prayers for her:
and what the living would then do.

such scenes do not take a person
closer to what might be a reason
for the final bit of fake,
kinships are pinned on sleeves
as coloured-cloth emblems
showing the mourners' grief,
joss-sticks and red candles
cannot give feeling to this meaning.
at cheng meng
do we offer ghosts the season's greetings?

fear of the known

they also belonged to the track:
the trees and banks of grass
flowing away from his notice,
the terrain slid by
heaving its periphery
then stabilised at the station.
getting off the train
and knowing he wouldn't be met
it still seemed strange
that needed were bustling people
to complete his desolation.

now burnt down
the house also belonged to him,
so he told of his departure
and waxed silent over a future
which will shuttle
to and fro
with remembrances and people
harrowing the alleys of bone

readjustment

after being educationally years away
he returned
expecting us to have remained ourselves.
we expected the mod suit
which he wore
and only that didn't belong here
(otherwise he was himself).

we'll listen to his talk
show concern, create some problems
offer our solutions
to prevent the rise of questions
which might need readjustment.
and only these do not belong here.

when it happens
we cannot cover
our consoling smiles
or smile to ourselves
that we are not torn
between a family and another country
then we know
we can't just go away
and drop our faces
to bridge the span
between our eyes and his heart

traces

see yourself by the sea
watching the tide roll tourists in
to ease the pull-out

and you will surely see
laden cars locked in glass
touring the city, splaying
much unwearied persistence.
those who are observant

see this backyard of poor families
leading to the question
after lear's fashion:
that as a dog, a rat has life
(not that these families lack any)
should it be lived so teemingly?
see also the situation
that it should be wanted
a dog's life, a rat's life.
then see again the question
and seeing no answer
trace the city
where traces are

certainty

you know a certain sureness
(not yours)
when the person cuts the air
with a crisp voice, very packed
for you to scratch a match
and light his cigarette
as he follows his voice past you.
then you find

(what a certain surprise)
he deplores style
detests trends,
he waves his hand
and topics end.
then his voice
amputating any diffidence
sprinkles over you
in tiny acid drops

a hot day

on a hot day i think
everything is an accident
and things being what they aren't
i have sometimes stood along
corridors and seen the world
spinning on its axis

and the child's distant balloon
is a little globe
attached to a string
with the bigger blue balloon
of the sky stretched behind

solitude

the street is blurred
lines and angles of solitude.
water runs a loose tent
to the drain and sea
returning to hang
wet over the street,
the houses
tired
carry still a load of that solitude

change of pace

today the sun tumbles out
scattering its spectrum wetly over grass
rushing children to play
on their weekly saturday.
the sun wears its fast 6 o'clock slant
and after today — who can say?

see how people change.

tomorrow there may be rain
pencilling briskly down
and the spectrum scattering.
what can we say
when the sun wears a 6 o'clock slant?

see now, people run

sunday

let me be glad if i see my thoughts
hang a mosquito-net over my head
burying me from inquiring existence:
the four corners one reliquary
till morning.
i should toss the net over my head
come out with one sudden thought:
how little ground i'll cover
to emerge to breakfast.

but this is sunday
without need to ask for knowledge
to found worlds
words to trigger profundity:
i hear my voice finding a thought
but do not question
create no simple guile
let me just lie
watching the day
with the morning
                    opening my window-sill

local colour

the artist himself is neither here nor there
he mistakes grassroots for his hair
now the strands have sprouted in the air
flanking an attap hut as a cultural stair

a scroll painting

the mountains are hazy with timeless passivity
sprawling monotonously in the left-hand corner
while clouds diffuse and fill the entire top half
before bumping daintily into a bright red parakeet
perched suicide-like on a beautifully gnarled branch
arched by the weight of fruit and one ripe peach
hung a motionless inch from the gaping beak

here is transient beauty
caught in permanence
but of what avail is such perpetual unattainment?

I know the stupid bird can never eat the stupid peach

we have silence

we have silence.
a silence bearing the arrogance
of the very inhibited
needs no decrepit words

but if it's this silence
then why don't you go away?

when you go
i am not so sure
you seek a motive for silence.
i seek a feeling for words
and find they come to me
dumb,
then they go
i am not sure
that i can see
in silence
you have no words
or are just dumb
eating me up

a letter

before the day closes again
on another inaction, the silence
of the road awaits your news for me.

you never arrived and each day
puts on new thoughts, spreads on new hopes
that your hands were run over
by a car. you could only sob the thoughts
feelings that i cannot hear. or that
there was no car. then, you have
no hands, anyway. you were ill, had
your lesson and heart-break. you
knowing that no one likes to open a letter
and find a piece of heartache
did not venture. i desiring to write again
thought only of you
of you: that it must move you
break you up, kill you.

the day your letter comes
i know it'll be full of news
and meaninglessness

departure

when you are away and this longing comes over
me, i let my thoughts run all over you
till you come back. it doesn't matter, not so much,
only a little of the quiet hysteria of your absence
remains
an awkward tickle
in the heart.

i laugh
but then i laugh out of nothing, out of spite
as you seem to have recalled
all the extensions and exultations
of your love, now, quickly folded up

while i, finding you retreating,
find it all points to me:
that what i have loved in you
retreats now in me,
you harbour no more love or grief

that you've left

that you have left, my eyes
make you sit with me in the sun
your toes drawn in folding sand.

the sea runs to sky
folding a still sun,
while knowing and feeling it all
you must still return to me
unfold as water breaks
shine like sun
wedge between my toes
as grains of sand

but evening must come
and we must move away

quick as a flash i must see again
this feeling, realise i've been
immersed in this idiocy of loss.
it isn't now july with the sun
these are rainy october days
grey afternoons filled with rain
which you disdain
and each day
situation and most of all
each person hasn't such clarity
the sun has, the sun shows
that beyond the clear sight of your eyes
you are blind

cameron highlands

1.

The road leads
not to clouds in the sky
only mists in a race
vying in ability to merge
as one fluid whole distinguished
by shades of purple-grey

on one side
the cliffs are 100 feet drops

2.

at the end of this road
beyond cabbages and farms
let me think ahead,
but not too much
i know i cannot ring
like an alarm clock

3.

it is here that a person
becomes a bare statement,
nothing seems very real
except what lies ahead unseen

balancing sounds

(not unusual) but early
brinchang rekindles activity
a 9 p. m. prelude
to the town's deep sleep
not many minutes later

silence walks down the road
under a bright patch of cloud
nesting in tall treetops
and a star hangs not far
picking faintly out
the white roadline
left side you are

coming back
to tanah rata,
hear its output of dogs
bark away the silence so far
so close, retreating
up again the misty road
shivering 4 miles back to brinchang

seasonal

soft-pawing the sky
are splayed leaves,
otherwise they're falling down:

ancient wind

swells this garden like a balloon
every minute blown larger
until it's about to burst:

ancient season
fascinates. we can't take
our eyes away
though it is not quite there

every casualty is happy
mindless in an abstract way
tracing where the wind ends
and it is right here
(we're the aftermath next month).
where it began, we were there:
ancient monsoon

ARTHUR YAP is one of Singapore's most important poets. He published four major collections of poetry: *only lines* (1971), *commonplace* (1977), *down the line* (1980), and *man snake apple & other poems* (1986). Of these four, *only lines*, *down the line*, and *man snake apple & other poems* all won the National Book Development Council award for poetry. He also contributed a section of poetry to *Five Takes* (1974), a publication featuring Chung Yee Chong, Sng Boh Khim, Yeo Bock Cheng, and Robert Yeo. Other awards included the Southeast Asian Writers Award (1983) and the Montblanc-National University of Singapore Center for the Arts Literary Award for English (1998).

Known also as a painter, Arthur Yap held exhibitions locally and abroad. In 1983, he was awarded the Cultural Medallion for his contributions to literature in Singapore, and from 1992 to 1996, he served as a creative writing mentor for the Creative Arts Program under the aegis of the Ministry of Education. Arthur Yap obtained his PhD in Linguistics from the National University of Singapore in 1982, and taught at the Department of English Language and Literature there until 1998. He passed away in 2006 at the age of 63.

JENNY YAP is sister of Arthur Yap, and she manages his literary estate. She was trained as a nurse in the UK, after which she worked in hospitals both in the UK and Singapore for over thirty years. She is now retired and volunteers at a local hospital.

IRVING GOH obtained his PhD in Comparative Literature from Cornell University and has served as Postdoctoral Research Fellow at the Society for the Humanities also at Cornell. He is currently Visiting Scholar at the Society. His book, *The Reject: From Contemporary French Thought to "Post-Secular" and "Posthuman" Futures*, is forthcoming with Fordham University Press. He is a former student of Arthur Yap.